D0040837

Literacy and Learning

Literacy and Learning

REFLECTIONS ON WRITING, READING, AND SOCIETY

Deborah Brandt

JOSSEY-BASS
A Wiley Imprint
www.josseybass.com

Library of Congress Cataloging-in-Publication Data

Brandt, Deborah, date
Literacy and learning : reflections on writing, reading, and society/by Deborah Brandt.
    p. cm.
    Includes bibliographical references and index.
    ISBN 978-0-470-40134-7 (cloth)
        1. Literacy—United States.   2. Literacy—Social aspects—United States.   3. Literacy—Economic aspects—United States.   4. Language arts—United States.   I. Title.
    LC151.B719   2009
    302.2'2440973—dc22

2008041912

Printed in the United States of America
FIRST EDITION
HB Printing   10 9 8 7 6 5 4 3 2 1

Outstanding Ideas in Education

The Outstanding Ideas in Education series offers an introduction to some of the leading thinkers in the field of education. Each volume provides a thought-provoking retrospective of their work—in their own words—through seminal articles and essays. In presenting these monumental ideas in a clear and comprehensive format, each volume in the series is designed to stimulate discussion and further innovation in the field.

In memory of Marilyn Sternglass

CONTENTS

INTRODUCTION

Writing at the Speed of Change

At the turn of the twentieth century, Calvin Lockett worked as a dispatcher with the Rutland Railroad. Among his duties was to send and receive messages via the telegraph regarding the routes and progress of the daily trains. He also set the semaphores with their colored signals—green, red, and yellow that would tell the train engineers how to proceed through the local station: whether to stop, go, or in the case of a yellow signal, to slow down for a message. The yellow signal meant that Lockett had written out a train order that would typically tell a south- or northbound train to get off the main track to make way for a train approaching from the opposite direction. After writing out the train order (an original and two carbon copies), Lockett would attach a copy to a spring-held hoop and, as the train slowed into the depot, he would hoist the hoop to the open window of the engine car. The engineer would reach out of the window, grab the hoop, remove the paper message, and throw the hoop back out the window of the moving train. In the meantime, Lockett would run along the tracks, sometimes as far as two hundred yards, pick up the hoop, dash back to the station, and insert a second copy of the train order into the hoop in time for the conductor at the back of the train to grab his copy as the caboose was passing by.

A communication system involving hoops and sprinting dispatchers seems humorously primitive from the perspective of today's networked communication. Yet for anyone interested in the arc of literacy over the last hundred years or so, this scene carries in its details many of the incipient forces that would keep Americans running to stay abreast of the moving train of change. All of the elements are here. They begin with industrialization and the crisis in information it created. As factories mass-produced more and more items for sale in shorter and shorter amounts of time and as trains sped them to storage or retail destinations on increasingly congested rail lines, old methods of communication proved inadequate. Enter technology as a remedy, in this case, the telegraph, which created national networks for sharing product information, controlling inventory, and, especially important to the railroad, providing internal coordination critical for safety and efficiency. Then, in the middle add a third element: the mental and scribal skills of American workers, in this case, in the figure of Calvin Lockett, whose fine penmanship (learned at school) and knowledge of Morse code (learned at the side of the station manager) became as necessary to the whole process as the steam engine.

This scene at a Vermont train station is also telling for what it anticipates: how vulnerable literacy skills would become as they got bound up with economic competition and technological change. By the 1940s, Calvin Lockett was out of work, the railroad was in receivership, and the need for telegraphers and fine penmen was nearing its end. As ways of working come and go, so too do the literacy practices associated with them, deflating the worth and reach of even sophisticated literacy skills. Today, Calvin Lockett's son—who had learned Morse code as a boy at the kitchen table with the plan of following in his father's footsteps—works in the marketing division of a national corporation, coordinating a regional sales team by e-mail and routing merchandise through strokes on a keyboard.

The economy's appetite for ever more productive communication suggests a different perspective on the nation's so-called literacy crisis. While it is common to lament the failure of some young people and adults to grasp "the basics" of reading and writing, we often forget that what is basic to one generation often proves inadequate for the next. In fact, relentless rounds of economic competition—increasingly waged on the grounds of knowledge production and communication—mean standards for literacy are always rising and our supply of literacy is in perpetual shortfall. The crisis is less about a lack and more about the gaps created as once viable forms of literacy are being rendered obsolete, or when once serviceable levels of literacy are being rendered uncompetitive, or when people's literacy potentials are going unrealized and unrewarded. Indeed, for many Americans living through these rapid transformations and faced repeatedly with new learning, the crisis appears more as a surplus than a deficit as sets of new literacy practices pile up on top of old ones and nothing ever quite goes away. Above all, this perspective asks us to appreciate why literacy and literacy learning are put at risk in the context of economic disruption and injustice. As investments in a community drain away and ways of working and living fade in value and influence, so too go the ways by which forms of literacy were practiced and learned as well as the ways by which they could connect to a wider society. Like idled railroad tracks pulled from their beds, once familiar routes to access and reward for literacy disappear. Finally, it must be remembered that the turbulence and instability brought to literacy by rapid economic change—including the gaps, accumulations, sudden inadequacies, and inequalities in access—create the context in which new literacy learners (young children, immigrants, and others) face the challenges of taking on literacy. That is, the task today is not merely to learn new forms of reading and writing but to do so in unprecedented conditions of complexity and uncertainty and under harsher consequences for failure. Needless to say, this puts difficult pressures on teachers, families, communities, and most of all, learners.

The growing entanglement of literacy with economic productivity not only affects how reading and writing are learned and practiced. It also shapes the rationales for acquiring literacy, how it is understood, valued, and evaluated. When Calvin Lockett, for example, learned handwriting in a rural school in the late-nineteenth century, having a "fine hand" was associated with decorum, discipline, character, in other words, moral qualities that linked mass literacy with its original projects of assimilation and civic training. But in rail depots and Western Union offices of the early twentieth century, handwriting was redeployed and redefined as a production skill, valued now for clarity, efficiency, and especially speed. Some telegraphers even learned to write with both hands at the same time, so that they could decode a message coming over the wire while simultaneously ticking off boxes and entering data on the message forms! Of course, moral connotations still cling to handwriting as they do to other elements of literacy. But in the transformation from a moral imperative to a production imperative, what was "good" about literacy underwent shifts.

Over the past fifteen years I have collected in-depth accounts from more than 150 people recollecting how they learned to read and write across their lifetimes, how they have used writing and reading in and out of work, how they value literacy, how they adapt to changes around literacy and how their experiences affect their families. The people I have interviewed have ranged in age from ninety-nine to ten and are diverse by race and ethnicity, education and income, religious affiliation and occupation. Collectively they learned literacy in such places as a shtetl in pre–World War One Poland; a refugee camp in post–Vietnam War Thailand; a segregated "side school" in Noxubee County, Mississippi, at mid-century; a kindergarten classroom that in 1975 was already computer-networked to Stanford University; a prison under the shifting rehabilitation policies of the 1980s and 1990s; and in living rooms, playgrounds, work sites, community centers, libraries, churches, union halls, military bases, shops, schools, and other locations across urban, rural, and suburban settings. Needless to say, the recollected scenes of reading and writing were eye-opening to me, most of all in the way that they teemed with references to people and things who seemed ever present and involved: parents, teachers, religious figures, military officers, older relatives or friends, authors, prison personnel, supervisors, physicians, therapists, librarians, product companies, government agencies, unions, school clubs, civil rights organizations, businesses and corporations, radio and television programs of all kinds, as well as an array of materials from ballpoint pens to newspapers, phonographs to appointment calendars, toys to computers that were sold, given, or issued at various times to the people I talked with.

So ubiquitous, diverse, and often rivalrous were these agents hovering at the scenes of literacy learning that I came to pay systematic attention to them. I came to think of them as *sponsors of literacy*. Sponsors are agents, local or distant, abstract or concrete, who enable, support, teach, model, recruit, regulate, suppress, or withhold literacy and gain advantage by it in some way. Sponsors of any kind, as we know, lend their resources or credibility to the sponsored, but do so for their own material or symbolic advantage, whether by direct repayment or, indirectly, by credit of association. Whenever anybody is learning to read or write anything, it is always possible to ask who is subsidizing the event and who besides the learner is benefitting. Sponsors are those agents who want our literacy as much as we do. They pursue us for our literacy even as we are in pursuit of literacy. They are the catalysts of change around literacy and the source of the ideological accumulation and congestion that grows up around it. Sponsors of literacy proliferated mightily over the last hundred years, particularly as "human capital" became more integral to economic production and profit. As sponsors compete with each other for dominance, they often use our literacy as the grounds of competition as they try to gain the upper hand. What we feel as the rising standards for literacy achievement—the demand on more and more people at younger and younger ages to do more and more things with symbols—reflects the fierce competitions in which literacy, especially now, gets caught up.

In paying attention to the role of the economy in shaping systems for literacy experience, I do not mean to imply that people value reading and writing only in terms of work and practicality. Nor do I advocate that teachers teach to such narrow interests. If anything, people's testimonies attest to the deep personal valuing of literacy for dignity, connection, continuity, development, faith, pleasure, action, and legacy. They also attest to the ingenious ways that people appropriate and redirect literacy learning for their own purposes. What I do argue is that the role of the economy must be approached critically as it is so influential in shaping systems of access and reward for literacy learning, for setting the material and ideological conditions in which literacy can be pursued and practiced, and for creating upheaval in those conditions. Teachers and learners as well as policy setters need these critical perspectives to function well. I also want to argue that just as schools are often called to account by business in the area of literacy achievement, businesses should better appreciate the role they play in helping and hurting literacy learning and be more accountable for it.

The essays in this volume capture shifts in the ways that literacy has been practiced, learned, and valued by everyday Americans over the last one hundred years. The essays themselves have been written over a period of fifteen years during which communication practices have been utterly transformed by the rise of the personal computer and especially the Internet. Indeed, most of the interviews were conducted prior to 1995 and already seem quaint in my eyes. The essays also carry the shifts and consolidations in my own thinking as I have continued to work with the in-depth interview as a method of inquiry and the idea of sponsorship as an explanatory concept for changes in literacy.

This volume is a mix of previously published essays (edited for this occasion), as well as previously unpublished talks, and new work, as well as a final excerpt from the conclusion of *Literacy in American Lives*. I thank *College English, College Composition and Communication, Written Communication,* and Cambridge University Press for permission to reprint material here. Special thanks go to Allan Dittmer for his continuing support and to Kate Gagnon at Jossey-Bass for her encouragement and attentiveness throughout the production of this volume. Thanks, finally, to all the folks in south-central Wisconsin, past, present, and future, who continue to agree to be interviewed as part of my ongoing investigations into literacy and learning in the society around me. Your patience, good nature, candor, and self-reflection are the real power behind the ideas of this volume.

THE GRAWEMEYER AWARD IN EDUCATION

A Conversation with Deborah Brandt

IN APRIL 2003, DEBORAH BRANDT TRAVELED TO THE UNIVERSITY OF LOUISVILLE to receive the Grawemeyer Award in Education for *Literacy in American Lives,* a book that traces the changing conditions for literacy learning across the twentieth century. As part of the ceremonies, Brandt sat down for a public conversation with then State Senator David Karem, who served as a member of the final award selection committee. The conversation took place at the Ekstrom Library on the University of Louisville campus. Members of the Charles Grawemeyer family, including Nancy Robbins, Martha Colton, and Marian James, were in attendance along with faculty and students from the University of Louisville, public school administrators and teachers, and members of the general public. The event began with a welcome and introductions from Allan Dittmer, professor of education at the University of Louisville and chair of the Grawemeyer Award committee. The session ended with questions from the audience. Here is an edited version of that conversation:

Allan Dittmer: Before we get started, it's a great honor to recognize the daughters of Charlie Grawemeyer, who are in the audience today. I had the great pleasure of talking with them about their dad when we wrote *The Power of Ideas,* a book about the awards. What a marvelous family and a wonderful father. It is a pleasure to introduce Deborah Brandt, author of *Literacy in American Lives,* a marvelously accessible book that garnered strong praise from members of the selection committee. Here are a few of the comments: "This book is a wonderful read. It teases something significant out of stories." "This is a hugely consequential book: a creative, organized study that spans four generations and extracts important insights from personal stories." "It expands the definition of literacy to look at the growing complexity of literacy sponsorship." And finally, one said, "This could become an American classic." Our format today is meant to be a little less formal and more spontaneous than the typical lecture. Deborah will be interviewed by one of the members of the selection committee, State Senator David Karem, So let's begin. It is my pleasure to introduce you to David Karem and Deborah Brandt, the recipient of the 2003 Graweyemer Award in Education.

David Karem: Let me begin by reminding everybody about the purpose of the University of Louisville Grawemeyer Award in Education. It is "to stimulate the dissemination, public scrutiny, and implementation of ideas that have potential to bring about significant improvement in educational practice and advances in educational attainment." From being on the selection committee and from reading the book and participating in all the discussions, what excited me about this book is that it met each and every one of those criteria. If people seize on this book, it really does have the opportunity to change some perspectives and perceptions.

I think it would be helpful, Deborah, if you just tell us a little about yourself, and then I think the audience would be interested in your perceptions about the Grawemeyer Award. How did you get to know about it?

DB: Before I start, I would like to thank my hosts here in Louisville. I am having a wonderful time. Thanks especially to Allan Dittmer, who has just been great in showing me around and getting me settled. Thanks to Stephanie Hilpp, who did a lot of the ground work to put this event together. I'm honored that there are members of the Grawemeyer family here. That's awesome to me. And I have had a wonderful time communicating with David Karem. If every legislator had his insights and commitment to education, our schools would be much better off right now.

I find it hard to talk about myself. I grew up in Southern New Jersey at the bottom of the Pine Barrens, inland from the coast. I am a pure product of public education, all the way through—K–12 in Vineland, New Jersey, and then on to my state university, Rutgers, where I was among the first women admitted to the all-male Rutgers College campus in 1972. After college I worked for a couple of years as a newspaper reporter. I did a lot of interviewing and learned this method of getting people to open up and talk. Then I was transplanted to the Midwest to do graduate work, M.A. and Ph.D., at Indiana University in a new field called composition or writing studies. Although I went to Indiana to study literature, I became more interested in the teaching of writing and in researching writing in the context of literacy—both the history and processes of literacy. After receiving my Ph.D. in 1983, I joined the faculty at the University of Wisconsin–Madison, and I have been there ever since. I teach undergraduate writing at all levels, freshmen to seniors. I teach a course for future English teachers. We have a graduate program in rhetoric and writing studies, and I teach courses in contemporary writing theory and literacy studies. My husband and I have a son who is a graduate of the University of Wisconsin–Madison and is attending NYU Law School.

DK: And can you talk about the Grawemeyer Award?

DB: Right. I became aware of the Grawemeyer Award by reading great books that I would have been reading anyway—work by people I admire so much, Mike Rose, Shirley Brice Heath, Victoria Purcell-Gates, Vanessa Walker. These are books that I would have encountered in my pursuit of understanding literacy and pedagogy and the history of education. Then there were those works in cross-fields by Howard Gardner and Carol Gilligan. *The Shape of the River* was a very important book for me because of my involvement with affirmative action on my campus. So I kept noticing this Grawemeyer Award, and I didn't really know what it was and I finally decided to find out. So I went to the Web site and learned the details. But I became aware of it through the work and the stature of the work that had received this award. So when Cambridge University Press said they wanted to nominate the book for some awards and would I provide a list of possibilities, I put the Grawemeyer Award on the list—even though it seemed like quite a dream to me at the time (and still does!). In any case, I do believe the Grawemeyer Award is getting much more known by more and more people. I hear it discussed in educational circles. I can tell you that after the award was announced, I heard from so many old colleagues, friends, and students from across the country, people I had lost track of who wrote to congratulate me about the award. It was one of the best things about this process. So it seems to me the award is growing in recognition and becoming part of the multidisciplinary field of education.

DK: The format of *Literacy in American Lives* is quite wonderful. Legislators deal with people and social issues on a daily basis. People write us letters, and that's interesting. People file petitions, and that's interesting. People provide statistics. But when somebody brings the human face to a problem, it really makes us get in touch with it. So the format of your book involves really in-depth interviews with people, and they really personalize the issues around literacy. I would like you to talk about how you came up with that format and things you found out from it.

DB: This all began innocently in a course I taught for future English teachers. We were reading a lot of theory and research about how people become literate, how they learn to write, and about the best ways to teach writing. And I wanted the students to have something of their own with which to interact with this material, to trouble it or interrogate it. So I simply gave each of them a sheet of paper with the question at the top: How did you learn to write? I asked them to remember spontaneously everything they could. I didn't know what was going to come back but immediately when I read the accounts I could see an incredible richness of detail, of historical specificity, regional specificity. They reported so much learning that was going on outside of school. Students remembered interacting with all sorts of materials—many already out of date and vanished. They uncovered rich aspects of literacy learning that, in my view, had simply not been recorded enough. If you look at how historians try to piece together the story of how literacy came to ordinary people, they often have to use indirect means. They have to look at signature rates or library circulation or the occasional journal or autobiography in which people talk about their literacy. I thought, well, here we are at the end of the twentieth century. Let's not let another century go by without trying to capture a process that is not often written down. So I wanted to expand the collection of accounts beyond just students in my classes. I toyed originally with going out and asking people to write their accounts, but then I realized that would exclude a lot of people who maybe couldn't write that much or would not have been comfortable or willing to do it. So I fell back on my old reporter instincts and decided to get at it through interviewing. So between roughly 1990 and 1995, I interviewed nearly a hundred people, even though I used only eighty in the book. They were all living at the time in Dane County, Wisconsin, where I live and work. I relied on schools, community organizations, labor unions, senior citizen centers, churches and synagogues, housing managers, and my own social and professional networks to locate people, some of whom were born and raised in Wisconsin, but others who came from many other parts of the country and some who were born outside of the United States and immigrated here. They were diverse in terms of race, ethnicity, schooling, region of birth, language heritage, religion, and occupation. And they ranged in age from ninety-nine to ten years old. I sat down with them usually in their homes, sometimes at work. Some of these interviews took place at the sides of hospital beds. I interviewed one man who, as it turned out, was in the last week of his life. Most of the interviews lasted between one and three hours. The longest went five-and-a-half. But that was rare. I asked people pretty methodically to remember everything they could about how they learned both to read and write. I have to say that many of the people I interviewed were initially puzzled by why I was interested in their reading and writing. They claimed they couldn't remember very much, and they weren't going to be a good interview. But in fact once we got talking, much as in my students' narratives, the rich, specific memories came out.

So I had all of these interviews that had to be analyzed. I had to figure out a systematic way to study them so that I could make claims or assert explanations about the changing conditions of literacy learning. I knew that the experiences of people born at the turn of the century were quite different from the stories I was getting from the younger people. I knew that there were differences within generations and that occupations, economics, region, histories of discrimination all were going to factor in. Even people who were the same age were acquiring literacy in quite different ways. So I used a method called grounded theory. It's a way of looking carefully, line by line, at the details of people's accounts, breaking down episodes from various lives and putting them into categories. I did strong comparison, sometimes case by case, across cohorts, and within categories, and I started seeing patterns about how literacy was changing and what was spurring this on. I also could see how people were coping with these changes. Only after many years—I think I spent six years working with this data—did I arrive at satisfactory generalizations that went across a lot of cases. Then I found individual accounts of people whose lives best exemplified or embodied those trends that were true of many, many lives. And that's how the form of this book came about. In several chapters I just treat a couple of people in depth. Or in one case, four generations of one family, or eight members of the same church. But their lives stood for the patterns I was seeing across the century.

DK: So the one family you interviewed, the great-grandmother was Genna May and the great-grandson was Michael May. And here is a statement out of the book that I thought was quite intriguing, and I hope you will comment on it:

> For members of the community in which Genna May grew up, the ability to write the words of everyday life often marked the end of formal schooling, whereas for Michael May [Genna's great-grandson] these same experiences served as a preparation for kindergarten.

When you really think about that, that's an incredibly powerful change in four generations. That one jumped out on me. Can you talk about it?

DB: Genna May was born in 1898 on a dairy farm in south-central Wisconsin. She attended a school that her parents helped to build, physically, on land that they donated to the school district, which was not uncommon. School was held fifteen weeks a year. She said she did little writing at home or at school, but when it occurred, she used a slate and chalk. The slates were at school and at home. There was little paper available in her rural area. Paper was reserved for her father's church work. He was a deacon in a Lutheran Church, and his literacy almost exclusively was for church writing. So she remembered these slates. They were crucial to her. She started school when she was seven years old. She spoke no English when she started school. She could not read or write when she started at seven years old, but learned at school and went on to be the first one in her family to finish high school, which was a monumental achievement in her family. Then I interviewed her eleven-year-old great-grandson who was attending a twenty-five-room middle school in a suburb of Madison, Wisconsin, where more than half the population had college degrees. Michael remembered first writing when he was two years old. He was in the family TV room, and his parents were showing him how to form words with those magnetic letters on an easel—kind of slate-like. In some concrete ways, his initiation into forming letters was not unlike his great-grandmother's. But it was occurring in a context that was so changed. The meanings of literacy had become so different, and his viability in the world was so tied up with literacy that those early, simple lessons were carrying a lot of meaning, including pressure to perform. I argue in the book that learning to read and write now is much harder because of all the different interpretations that have to go into it and the higher standards associated with it. Some people argue that there was a golden age of literacy when people used to be much more literate. I have to tell you, based on the accounts I collected, that wasn't the case. By the time he was eleven, Michael May had written research reports, poems, short stories, a letter to the editor, a plan for draining water from his school playground; he kept a journal and exchanged birthday cards with his great-grandmother. He used slates, chalk, pencil, pens, paper, a typewriter, and a computer to write. Studying four generations of one family who stayed in the same part of the country over the course of one hundred years helped me track the rising standards for literacy achievement and the changing regional economy that was pressuring those standards to rise.

DK: It seems to me important for folks to understand about this book—you have told us the methodology, dig a little different. Why did you do the book? You know, all legislators are cynical, so was there some preconceived thesis you were trying to prove?

DB: I wish I had! In other words, I wish I knew when I started what I knew when I finished because I would have asked more pointed questions. I was probing with this project. I wanted to fill in things that historians of literacy told us weren't available in earlier centuries. I said: Let's find out what happened in the twentieth century. To formulate the interview questions, I used what I knew about the history of literacy, how literacy had come to people in the past, and the institutions that were involved. I wanted to see if and how those early literacy institutions continued to matter in the pursuit of literacy. As part of that probe, I asked about work-related literacy. As it turned out, work became really central in explaining the changes that were going on around literacy. I hadn't really anticipated that. I was interested in what was propelling change and what was contributing to inequities in literacy and what ordinary people were doing to keep up with these changes or to deal with these inequities. It turned out that economic change, our transformation from agriculture to manufacturing to information, was the incentive for a lot of literacy learning—sometimes agreeably and sometimes because people really didn't have any choice. As our economy changed, literacy got pulled into production processes, and people's literacy skills became the way that wealth got produced and economic competitions were won or lost. But I really had no idea that that was going to be so important. If I had, if I could do it over again, I would have asked many more questions and more pointed questions about literacy and work. But most broadly I simply wanted to capture a part of the history of literacy from the perspective of ordinary people. And I wanted to make sure I kept their perspectives in whatever answers I came up with. And that was how the book got written. What became the central concept of the book was what I called *sponsors of literacy*—agents, forces, and institutions that stimulated people's literacy for their own economic or political or cultural advantage. In the twentieth century, sponsors of literacy proliferated, and their competitions with and for the skills of the American people accelerated change around literacy and raised the stakes around it.

DK: I'd like to jump into another area, and this has to do with the African American community. One statement you make in the book that I should have understood, but it just never entered my mind is that: "Black churches were the only institutions in America that were free from white domination. Consequently Black churches provided not only a space for the development of theological views but also an opportunity for Black people's leadership skills to develop and for frank expression and exchange. In the absence of competing institutions, Black churches typically took on many more worldly social functions than did mainstream religious institutions. Chief among these social functions, both before and after Emancipation, were the teaching of literacy and the building and staffing of schools." The importance of Black churches should have been quite evident to me, but that they were places free of white domination where there could be this interchange is a wonderful piece of the book.

DB: Well, those observations come from the historical and sociological work of James D. Anderson, Janet Cornelius, W.E.B. DuBois, V. P. Franklin, Gilbert Anthony Williams, and others. What I tried to add was the idea of sponsors of literacy. I tried to understand how that history of the Black church worked according to the idea of sponsorship and how that legacy ran through the lives of people I interviewed. I talked to twenty African Americans born between 1914 and 1978, and eight of them were members of the same African Methodist Episcopal Church. I attended the church as a way of understanding what they were telling me about their literacy. As I just said, one of the arguments of the book is that what stands behind our learning to read and write are what I call *sponsors*. They are agents who have vested interests, maybe even ulterior motives in our learning to read and write, agents who provide opportunities for learning but in doing so, shape our experiences with literacy. In the early stages of mass literacy in the United States, those sponsors were largely Protestant churches, who used literacy to convert people to their beliefs. Many African Americans, even before Emancipation, learned to read and write through the church (that is, when state laws or slaveholders weren't forbidding it). Through the late-nineteenth and early-twentieth century, many more literacy sponsors came into prominence in the White population, particularly economic sponsors interested in literacy for consumption and production. But African Americans were still locked out of the wider society and the schooling and jobs that went along with it. White society did not care so much about the development of the literacy skills of African Americans and did not provide much reward for literacy even for African Americans who achieved high levels of literacy. So the Black church continued its long-standing mission as a site for literacy and literacy development to thrive and kept that going across the twentieth century. This has given a different cultural character to African American literacy over time. If, in White society, there was a proliferation and diffusion of literacy sponsors and a secularizing of the values of literacy, in the Black church we find a single literacy sponsor that took on a proliferation of functions and kept literacy strongly associated with spirituality and personhood.

This legacy was still evident in a Wisconsin A.M.E. church of the 1990s. The minister of the church acted as a literacy teacher. He instructed adults and children in the writing of essays that they would present as part of their leadership turns at prayer meetings or in Sunday school or for marking religious holidays or special occasions in African American history. Several people I interviewed were working on drafts of these essays at the time I was interviewing them, drafts that they would share with the minister to get constructive criticism. They used the minister's library for source material. He had concordances and Bibles. They used his photocopying machine. He was making those provisions. Some people were writing in connection with their involvement with housing issues in the community because the church was involved in housing projects, and members of the church sat on various advisory boards. This congregation even used writing during the worship service, something I have never seen in White Methodist services. The congregation had something called the Burden Box, and at a particular stage in the service, people were invited to get out paper and pens and write down their burdens and place them in the box. For several minutes, the service just stopped and everybody wrote. It was a way of healing, a way of letting go and going on. Also during the service, church members actively participated in intense discussion of Bible readings. The preacher was not the only person speaking or the only person offering analysis. People rose and spoke and analyzed texts from the pews, often mixing in observations and experiences from their own lives. It was like a school seminar. Also during the service, they took up a collection for their Education Fund, a bit of money that helped pay for school supplies for young people who were in school or in college. So I saw in this church a sponsor who was nurturing the congregation at every level, spiritually, economically, educationally, politically, and it's a different . . . I don't want to call it older because the people of the church were not living in the past. Many worked in high-tech jobs, including the minister. But there is this older trend and tradition that makes literacy in that church more valuable when it is doing more than one thing, when it has spiritual worth, political worth, personhood worth. I wish schools and other agencies would recognize the different cultural legacies around literacy and bring these meanings more regularly into the ways that reading and writing are used in school, meanings like literacy needs to be practical and uplifting and emancipatory at the same time. Those meanings resonate with many African American children and parents as a result of history and tradition.

DK: To me, the central theme of the book has to do with the following quote, which I will ask you to talk about. I think this is one of the things that could really spark controversy: "As democratic institutions, schools are supposed to exist to offset imbalances that market philosophy helps to create, including especially imbalances in the worth of people's literacy. The more that the school organizes literacy teaching and learning to serve the needs of the economic system, the more it betrays its democratic possibilities. The more that private interests take over the education and development of our young citizens, the less of a democracy we have." Deborah, that's a pretty far-reaching statement. That's a tough statement that you make.

DB: First, I want to be clear that this is me speaking at the end. In the conclusion I come out and speak for myself about the findings. It is not something the interviewees said, and I imagine some of them might disagree with me. But, as I told you, I am a product of public schooling, K through Ph.D. And when I became a teacher in a public school, I really tried to figure out what my role was. And I was influenced by the philosophy of John Rawls and his theory of justice. He makes the point that the world is filled with injustices. Some people get lucky breaks and some don't. Some people are born with fewer health problems than others. Some people are born in geographies that are bountiful and will give them lots of food, and other people will be born in places where it is harder to grow food. Some injustices are based on systematic discrimination by race, gender, religion, dialect. And we have an economic system of capitalism that thrives on making some people winners and some people losers. But as Rawls describes it and as I understand it, democratic institutions, public institutions that are supported by all of the people—whether they are healthy or sick, lucky or less lucky, free of discrimination or not, rich or poor—are the places with the obligation to make sure that the inequalities that are occurring are not so life-determining that there is hopelessness. This is the point of having democratic institutions and public schools to address those inequities through civil rights and equal education and democracy-promoting education so that people can overcome or reject inequity. Literacy has always been intimately connected to this project and to the well functioning of a democracy. We know that having an educated citizenry was an important aspect of democratic thought. And in a print society (or a post-print society now), our First Amendment rights, our freedom of speech, and the viability of our other rights are really linked up with literacy when you think about it. How can you have an effective voice in this society if your literacy is not protected and developed equally to others'? So literacy and literacy equality are linked to the First Amendment. Now especially with the economic changes that have occurred and the ways that literacy is entangled with economic productivity and global competition, we are under pressure—schools feel it, teachers in this room feel it certainly in the last couple of decades—to see literacy narrowly in terms of preparation for work and the sense that schools have to be accountable to business, meaning ever more skills, ever earlier reading and writing, and testing, testing, testing. This is the pressure from an economy that uses mental and scribal skills as its raw materials. And I think that is fine to a degree. We all have to make a living. But if this meaning of literacy overrides or takes over or obliterates the other responsibilities that the school has to protect and develop equitably the voices and experiences and representations and rights of all of our students, then we are not doing our job. So I would like to be able to talk back to industry now and remind them that we could never have had an information economy if we did not have a highly literate and highly skilled population. It wouldn't have happened. Schools should be being praised right now. Instead, schools are being made to feel that we can't keep up, we're not doing enough because we are being brought into those cycles of unending competition and winners and losers. I think we should remind the society that we do have these other responsibilities and that they don't always go in the same way that these economic interests are pushing us. These are very important functions. But attending to the relationship between literacy and civil rights is a responsibility that no other institution is responsible for except us, and if we don't perform it, if we don't sponsor it, everybody is going to lose out. Economic change brings new opportunities for literacy. But economic change also destroys older opportunities for literacy upon which some people are continuing to rely. It rips up the routes that people have to literacy. It rips up the cultural avenues that people had for literacy. I interviewed a lot of people who were in dying communities, and their literacy was not being sponsored. Nobody was picking them up. They were literate, but their skills were becoming less valued in the economy. And so I wanted to address teachers about what became so clear to me through these accounts. And I wanted to address industry about how its decisions create problems for literacy and literacy learning. Business needs more awareness of how much it is affecting literacy and literacy problems and take more responsibility. Accountability needs to be broadly shared.

DK: I'm glad you came out in the end and you made those points. I wish this book would be required reading for every member of the Kentucky General Assembly and for that matter every member of every General Assembly and some of the people in the federal

Congress because I find it terribly appealing that you make the statement that literacy needs to be addressed in the civil rights context. It's a powerful and important statement. I have a last question and then we will turn to the audience.

DB: But wait a minute. We are almost out of time, and I wanted to ask you about your earliest memories of literacy. One of the key questions in the interview was: What was your earliest memory of writing anything. I wondered if you have an early memory.

DK: My earliest memory. Well, I'm a product of a Roman Catholic school system in this community, and so my earliest memories of writing were laboriously handwriting little words down columns in very painful, tedious sorts of ways and not all that exciting. But were it about reading—my older brother used to get these pulp magazines about soldiers trapped on desert islands with fifteen beautiful women, and there were no pictures and so you really did have to read the articles!

DB: Yes, and you had to read very actively, very constructively too, right?

DK: And they were always under my brother's mattress for some reason.

DB: Well, I was going to analyze your memories, but maybe, for now, we should just let that go and turn to questions from the audience.

Question 1: What does the Grawemeyer Award mean to you financially?

DB: I am still stunned by it. I'm working through what it means financially. I do know that I will be able to gift off to the University. I teach in a precollege opportunity program for kids in Madison. Middle school kids. I know that I will be able to contribute some scholarship money there that will be important to me. I'll be able to start a new research project immediately—a little faster than

I thought. And I'll put the rest of it up and figure out what it is going to mean. But I do know psychologically it certainly raises the standards for the research that I will do in the future and for the work that I am doing with graduate students now.

DK: Could you at least treat yourself to a bottle of wine or something?

DB: My husband and I are from families of modest means, and we are frugal people. So this is a mind-boggling thing. There is probably a bottle of wine in there somewhere, though.

Question 2: How can teachers be prepared for teaching the multiliteracies that are springing up in society now?

DB: This is a really important question and goes right to the heart of the rapidity of change that I have been talking about. I first want to observe that I finished collecting interviews for *Literacy in American Lives* in 1995, and only a mere handful of the one hundred people I talked with—all young people—even had access to the Internet, and none of them was really anticipating its significance. So multiliteracies—the convergence of mass reading and mass writing with picture, sound, and motion made possible by computers and the Internet—are a new concept for the society and for teachers. How are these affordances changing what it means to compose now? Writers now have responsibilities they didn't have before. Everybody is writer, editor, illustrator, and publisher of their own work. You even have to find your own audiences. You have to control so many more processes as a part of routine composition. What are the basics of composition? I have little confidence that the genres we are using now and the ways we are arranging words and pictures and so on will be around twenty years from now. The technology will change. Standardization will set in. So what is important to teach? And there are terrifically difficult access issues, terrific difficulties for parents trying to teach their children literacy when they themselves weren't taught the forms that seem to matter now. I happen to think in circumstances like this that it is less important to teach the techniques and technology and more important to help students realize what is happening and what is happening to them. Writing, authoring, is now being afforded—and expected—on a mass scale. What are the responsibilities that come with authorship? Also, who is sponsoring our literacy and what do they want from it? I guess I am advocating for a set of approaches or dispositions, critical dispositions, by which students can understand what change around literacy means and what it means to take on authorship and that these understandings should accompany the technical aspects. But it is a terrific challenge for schools because they are generally underfinanced and underequipped, because so many teachers were educated in a different era, and because what we need to learn keeps proliferating. The old forms of literacy aren't going away. This is what I mean about the difficulty of learning to read and write now because so many multiple systems are present. Learning used to be about taking on the traditions of one's elders. That form of learning—particularly around literacy—is over. So I don't have a good answer to your question.

DK: I see kids getting into positive chat rooms and talking to one another, even at seven and eight years old. That's an intriguing form. They use games to communicate. They play word games long distance.

DB: We talked about this in Allan Dittmer's class last night: the kids are using keyboards to chat with each other. They are producing much more writing. But it's based not on reading but on talking. We will find a different kind of writing in the future. More kids are going directly into writing and are less steeped in reading—books, anyway. So that's going to be a new challenge for teachers and will change the kind of writing that we value in the future.

Question 3: In my grandchild's first-grade class, they are writing down all their thoughts for the day without regard to spelling. And at the end of the year they will make a book. What do you think?

DB: It is interesting to me how different this experience is from the one that David Karem recalled earlier. He spent the first grade learning to control handwriting. Your grandchild is learning how to be an author. In some ways I think this is a great way to start because at least you learn something about what writing is for, that it is a meaningful cultural practice, and it is more than just being correct. I talked to many people who were stymied all their lives in writing because they had these early, unhappy handwriting episodes. They thought they could not compose because their writing was sloppy or because they couldn't spell. So these are good innovations from my perspective if writing becomes a part of life one depends on and can call one's own. Eventually the correct spelling will come—probably when the writing is turned into a polished book. Of course, through the lens of sponsorship, we might see at the same time that your grandchild may already be being groomed to be a member of the creative class, where individuality and the importance of one's own ideas is cultivated as a way of inspiring innovation. Your grandchild is being groomed for productivity in a knowledge society or a communication society. This manner of literacy is not available in all of our first-grade classes; too often it is usually in professional communities where children are given the privilege of imagining this role for themselves.

Question 4: Can you comment on the sponsorship that lies behind the accountability and testing movement?

DB: I think we see a concern with future economic productivity. There are going to be a lot of old people and far fewer young people to support them. Someone told me that this nation has to increase its productivity by 14 percent or something like that to be sustainable—so that's a lot of pressure on today's youth. The youth will have to work at a level 14 percent higher than workers do now just to support the older generation. That's what we see in this No Child Left Behind movement—the need to squeeze value out of all the youngsters so that they can function in the economy as it is imagined in the future and not be a drag on society. There is a feeling that schools have to make sure that these students are going to be able to keep on learning and come out the other side ready for economic usefulness. We can't make that go away, but we could turn it around and make it work to our benefit. Certainly I would wish there would be more tax money raised from businesses who are the beneficiaries of a highly educated workforce and put back into the public schools, to make these higher standards more realistic. We also have inequities in the basic funding of schools, which is a terrible thing. I went back into all the presidential speeches to find mentions of the words *literacy* or *reading* or *writing*, and I couldn't find many mentions until very recently. But when you have President Clinton and President Bush both talking about third-grade reading scores, you know something is up. It's a productivity problem.

DK: You may be interested to know that in 1990 we passed major education reform, one of the most significant in the country, and got one of the Harvard American Innovation Awards for it. It's a fabulous thing. At that time the corporate community did step up and say we should pay our fair share for this to happen. And they did. We taxed them at the fair share they agreed to pay, and then as we left Frankfurt, they instantly hired a battery of lawyers who have gone very systematically through to see how they could diminish their share and form offshore corporations, out-of-state corporations so that their percentage has dropped significantly, probably about 50 percent from where they were at the time. Yet they are significant beneficiaries. Okay, so this will be our last question.

Question 5: I want to push you a little more on that last answer and think about the effect of accountability on writing in particular. This testing really favors a restrictive kind of literacy. It is not about a continual expansion of ever-greater dimensions of literacy. It seems more of a dumbing down of forms of literacy that have occurred in school previously. So it may be about economic production but not about more critical thinking, more literacy, but about containing literacy and making a compliant workforce.

DB: I agree with you. The application of these ideas is suffering under simplified notions of what literacy is. That's what we see in the testing and accountability models that are out there. When you read the business literature, they talk about critical thinking, fluid interpretation, and so on, but No Child Left Behind is itself very much behind in terms of the kinds of tests and curriculum it supports. There is a great mismatch. I think they are going to be struggling with that. Many of these models are going to be found unsatisfactory pretty soon. So I hear what you are saying.

DK: We are at the end of our time. It is important that we keep in mind the power of what Charles Grawemeyer has done for this community and that we all remember that and thank him not only in this field but in the various fields for which he has done benefit. We need to thank the Grawemeyer family. We are extraordinarily grateful. We thank Deborah for a work that we all need to read and treasure. You are about the business of changing lives and affecting young people. They are our greatest resource. You know that. We cannot tell you how grateful we are. We are challenged by your work. And thanks to the audience. Take away something from this and continue the good work that you do. All of us are about the business of helping one another.

DB: Thank you all so very much.

1

Sponsors of Literacy

IN HIS SWEEPING HISTORY OF ADULT LEARNING IN THE UNITED STATES, Joseph Kett describes the intellectual atmosphere available to young apprentices who worked in the small, decentralized print shops of antebellum America. Because printers also were the solicitors and editors of what they published, their workshops served as lively incubators for literacy and political discourse. By the mid-nineteenth century, however, this learning space was disrupted when the invention of the steam press reorganized the economy of the print industry. Steam presses were so expensive that they required capital outlays beyond the means of many printers. As a result, print jobs were outsourced, the processes of editing and printing were split, and, in tight competition, print apprentices became low-paid mechanics with no more access to the multiskilled environment of the craft shop (Kett, 1994, pp. 67–70). While this shift in working conditions may be evidence of the deskilling of workers induced by the Industrial Revolution (Nicholas and Nicholas, 1992), it also offers a site for reflecting upon the dynamic sources of literacy and literacy learning. The reading and writing skills of print apprentices in this period were the achievements not simply of teachers and learners or of the discourse practices of the printer community. Rather, these skills existed fragilely, contingently within an economic moment. The pre–steam press economy enabled some of the most basic aspects of the apprentices' literacy, especially their access to material production and the public meaning or worth of their skills. Paradoxically, even as the steam-powered penny press made print more accessible (by making publishing more profitable), it brought an end to a particular form of literacy sponsorship and a drop in literate potential.

The apprentices' experience invites rumination upon literacy learning and teaching today. Literacy looms as one of the great engines of profit and competitive advantage in the twentieth century: a lubricant for consumer desire; a means for integrating corporate markets; a foundation for the deployment of weapons and other technology; a raw material in the mass production of information. As ordinary citizens have been compelled into these economies, their reading and writing skills have grown sharply more central to the everyday trade of information and goods as well as to the pursuit of education, employment, civil rights, and status. At the same time, people's literate skills have grown vulnerable to unprecedented turbulence in their economic value, as conditions, forms, and standards of literacy achievement seem to shift with almost every new generation of learners. How are we to understand the vicissitudes of individual literacy development in relationship to the large-scale economic forces that set the routes and determine the worldly worth of that literacy? The field of writing studies has had much to say about individual literacy development. Especially in the last quarter of the twentieth century, we have theorized, researched, critiqued, debated, and sometimes even managed to enhance the literate potentials of ordinary citizens as they have tried to cope with life as they find it. Less easily and certainly less steadily have we been able to relate what we see, study, and do to these larger contexts of profit making and competition. This even as we recognize that the most pressing issues we deal with—tightening associations between literate skill and social viability, the breakneck pace of change in communications technology, persistent inequities in access and reward—all relate to structural conditions in literacy's bigger picture. When economic forces are addressed in our work, they appear primarily as generalities: contexts, determinants, motivators, barriers, and touchstones (but see Faigley, 1999; Miller, 1991; Spellmeyer, 1996). Rarely are they systematically related to the local conditions and embodied moments of literacy learning that occupy so many of us on a daily basis.

This chapter does not presume to overcome the analytical failure completely. But it does offer a conceptual approach that begins to connect literacy as an individual development to literacy as an economic development, at least as the two have played out over the last ninety years or so. The approach is through what I call sponsors of literacy. Sponsors, as I have come to think of them, are any agents, local or distant, concrete or abstract, who enable, support, teach, model, as well as recruit, regulate, suppress, or withhold literacy—and gain advantage by it in some way. Just as the ages of radio and television accustom us to having programs brought to us by various commercial sponsors, it is useful to think about who or what underwrites occasions of literacy learning and use.[1] Although the interests of the sponsor and the sponsored do not have to converge (and, in fact, may conflict) sponsors nevertheless set the terms for access to literacy and wield powerful incentives for compliance and loyalty. Sponsors are a tangible reminder that literacy learning throughout history has always required permission, sanction, assistance, coercion, or, at minimum, contact with existing trade routes. Sponsors are delivery systems for the economies of literacy, the means by which these forces present themselves to and through individual learners. They also represent the causes into which people's literacy usually gets recruited.[2]

For the last five years I have been tracing sponsors of literacy across the twentieth century as they appear in the accounts of ordinary Americans recalling how they learned to write and read. The investigation is grounded in more than one hundred in-depth interviews that I collected from a diverse group of people born roughly between 1900 and 1980. In the interviews, people explored in great detail their memories of learning to read and write across their lifetimes, focusing especially on the people, institutions, materials, and motivations involved in the process. The more I worked with these accounts, the more I came to realize that they were filled with references to sponsors, both explicit and latent, who appeared in formative roles at the scenes of literacy learning. Patterns of sponsorship became an illuminating site through which to track the different cultural attitudes people developed toward writing versus reading, as well as the ideological congestion faced by late-century literacy learners as their sponsors proliferated and diversified (see my essays on "Remembering Reading, Remembering Writing" and "Accumulating Literacy" [Brandt, 1994; Brandt, 1995]). In this chapter I set out a case for why the concept of sponsorship is so richly suggestive for exploring economies of literacy and their effects. Then, through use of extended case examples, I demonstrate the practical application of this approach for interpreting current conditions of literacy teaching and learning, including persistent stratification of opportunity and escalating standards for literacy achievement.

Sponsorship

Intuitively, sponsors seemed a fitting term for the figures who turned up most typically in people's memories of literacy learning: older relatives, teachers, priests, supervisors, military officers, editors, influential authors. Sponsors, as we ordinarily think of them, are powerful figures who bankroll events or smooth the way for initiates. Usually richer, more knowledgeable, and more entrenched than the sponsored, sponsors nevertheless enter a reciprocal relationship with those they underwrite. They lend their resources or credibility to the sponsored, but also stand to gain benefits from their success, whether by direct repayment or, indirectly, by credit of association (Bourne, 1986; Lynch, 1986; Hortsman and Kurtz, 1978). Sponsors also proved an appealing term in my analysis because of all the commercial references that appeared in these twentieth-century accounts—the magazines, peddled encyclopedias, essay contests, radio and television programs, toys, fan clubs, writing tools, and so on, from which so much experience with literacy was derived. As the twentieth century turned the abilities to read and write into widely exploitable resources, commercial sponsorship abounded.

In whatever form, sponsors deliver the ideological freight that must be borne for access to what they have. Of course, the sponsored can be oblivious to or innovative with this ideological burden. Like Little Leaguers who wear the logo of a local insurance agency on their uniforms, not out of a concern for enhancing the agency's image but as a means for getting to play ball, people throughout history have acquired literacy pragmatically under the banner of others' causes. In the days before free, public schooling in England, Protestant Sunday schools warily offered basic reading instruction to working-class families as part of evangelical duty. To the horror of many in the church sponsorship, these families insistently, sometimes riotously demanded of their Sunday schools more instruction, including in writing and math, because it provided means for upward mobility (Laqueur, 1976). Through the sponsorship of Baptist and Methodist ministries, African Americans in slavery taught each other to understand the Bible in subversively liberatory ways. Under a conservative regime, they developed forms of critical literacy that sustained religious, educational, and political movements both before and after emancipation (Cornelius, 1991). Most of the time, however, literacy takes its shape from the interests of its sponsors. And, as we will see here, obligations toward one's sponsors run deep, affecting what, why, and how people write and read. Over the last one hundred years or so, the competition to harness mass literacy, to manage, measure, teach, and exploit it, has intensified, setting the terms for individuals' encounters with literacy. This competition shapes the incentives and barriers (including uneven distributions of opportunity) that greet literacy learners in any particular time and place.

The concept of sponsors helps to explain, then, a range of human relationships and ideological pressures that turn up at the scenes of literacy learning—from benign sharing between adults and youths, to euphemized coercions in schools and workplaces, to the most notorious impositions and deprivations by church or state. In the next three sections, I trace the dynamics of literacy sponsorship through the life experiences of several individuals, showing how their opportunities for literacy learning emerge out of the jockeying and skirmishing for economic and political advantage going on among sponsors of literacy. Along the way, the analysis addresses three key issues: (1) how, despite ostensible democracy in educational chances, stratification of opportunity continues to organize access and reward in literacy learning; (2) how sponsors contribute to what is called "the literacy crisis," that is, the perceived gap between rising standards for achievement and people's ability to meet them; and (3) how encounters with literacy sponsors can be sites for the innovative rerouting of resources into projects of self-development and social change.

Sponsorship and Access

A focus on sponsorship can force a more explicit and substantive link between literacy learning and systems of opportunity and access. A statistical correlation between high literacy achievement and high socioeconomic, majority-race status routinely shows up in results of national tests of reading and writing performance (Applebee, Langer, and Mullis, 1986). These findings capture, yet in their shorthand way, obscure the unequal conditions of literacy sponsorship that lie behind differential outcomes in academic performance. Throughout their lives, affluent people from high-caste racial groups have multiple and redundant contacts with powerful literacy sponsors as a routine part of their economic and political privileges. Poor people and those from low-caste racial groups have less consistent, less politically secured access to literacy sponsors—especially to the ones that can grease their way to academic and economic success. Differences in their performances are often attributed to family background (namely, education and income of parents) or to particular norms and values operating within different ethnic groups or social classes. But in either case, much more is usually at work.

As a study in contrasts in sponsorship patterns and access to literacy, consider the parallel experiences of Raymond Branch and Dora Lopez, both of whom were born in 1969 and, as young children, moved with their parents to the same mid-sized university town in the Midwest.[3] Both were still residing in this town at the time of our interviews in 1995. Raymond Branch, a European American, had been born in Southern California, the son of a professor father and a real estate executive mother. He recalled that his first-grade classroom in 1975 was hooked up to a mainframe computer at Stanford University and that, as a youngster, he enjoyed fooling around with computer programming in the company of "real users" at his father's science lab. This process was not interrupted much when, in the late 1970s, his family moved to the Midwest. Raymond received his first personal computer as a Christmas present from his parents when he was twelve years old, and a modem the year after that. In the 1980s, computer hardware and software stores began popping up within a bicycle-ride's distance from where he lived. The stores were serving the university community and, increasingly, the high-tech industries that were becoming established in that vicinity. As an adolescent, Raymond spent his summers roaming these stores, sampling new computer games, making contact with founders of some of the first electronic bulletin boards in the nation, and continuing, through reading and other informal means, to develop his programming techniques. At the time of our interview he had graduated from the local university and was a successful freelance writer of software and software documentation, with clients in both the private sector and the university community.

Dora Lopez, a Mexican American, was born in the same year as Raymond Branch, 1969, in a Texas border town, where her grandparents, who worked as farm laborers, lived most of the year. When Dora was still a baby her family moved to the same Midwest university town as had the family of Raymond Branch. Her father pursued an accounting degree at a local technical college and found work as a shipping and receiving clerk at the university. Her mother, who also attended technical college briefly, worked part-time in a bookstore. In the early 1970s, when the Lopez family made its move to the Midwest, the Mexican American population in the university town was barely 1 percent. Dora recalled that the family had to drive seventy miles to a big city to find not only suitable groceries but also Spanish-language newspapers and magazines that carried information of concern and interest to them. (Only when reception was good could they catch Spanish-language radio programs coming from Chicago, 150 miles away.) During her adolescence, Dora Lopez undertook to teach herself how to read and write in Spanish, something, she said, that neither her brother nor her U.S.-born cousins knew how to do. Sometimes, with the help of her mother's employee discount at the bookstore, she sought out novels by South American and Mexican writers, and she practiced her written Spanish by corresponding with relatives in Colombia. She was exposed to computers for the first time at the age of thirteen when she worked as a teacher's aide in a federally funded summer school program for the children of migrant workers. The computers were being used to help the children to be brought up to grade level in their reading and writing skills. When Dora was admitted to the same university that Raymond Branch attended, her father bought her a used word-processing machine that a student had advertised for sale on a bulletin board in the building where Mr. Lopez worked. At the time of our interview, Dora Lopez had transferred from the university to a technical college. She was working for a cleaning company, where she performed extra duties as a translator, communicating on her supervisor's behalf with the largely Latina cleaning staff. "I write in Spanish for him, what he needs to be translated, like job duties, what he expects them to do, and I write lists for him in English and Spanish," she explained.

In Raymond Branch's account of his early literacy learning we are able to see behind the scenes of his majority-race membership, male gender, and high-end socioeconomic family profile. There lies a thick and, to him, relatively accessible economy of institutional and commercial supports that cultivated and subsidized his acquisition of a powerful form of literacy. One might be tempted to say that Raymond Branch was born at the right time and lived in the right place—except that the experience of Dora Lopez troubles that thought. For Raymond Branch, a university town in the 1970s and 1980s provided an information-rich, resource-rich learning environment in which to pursue his literacy development, but for Dora Lopez, a female member of a culturally unsubsidized ethnic minority, the same town at the same time was information and resource-poor. Interestingly, both young people were pursuing projects of self-initiated learning, Raymond Branch in computer programming and Dora Lopez in Spanish-English biliteracy. But she had to reach much further afield for the material and communicative systems needed to support her learning. Also, while Raymond Branch, as the son of an academic, was sponsored by some of the most powerful agents of the university (its laboratories, newest technologies, and most educated personnel), Dora Lopez was being sponsored by what her parents could pull from the peripheral service systems of the university (the mail room, the bookstore, the second-hand technology market). In these accounts we also can see how the development and eventual economic worth of Raymond

Branch's literacy skills were underwritten by late-century transformations in communication technology that created a boomtown need for programmers and software writers. Dora Lopez's biliterate skills developed and paid off much further down the economic reward ladder, in government-sponsored youth programs and commercial enterprises, that, in the 1990s, were absorbing surplus migrant workers into a low-wage, urban service economy.

Tracking patterns of literacy sponsorship, then, gets beyond SES shorthand to expose more fully how unequal literacy chances relate to systems of unequal subsidy and reward for literacy. These are the systems that deliver large-scale economic, historical, and political conditions to the scenes of small-scale literacy use and development. This analysis of sponsorship forces us to consider not merely how one social group's literacy practices may differ from another's, but how everybody's literacy practices are operating in differential economies, which supply different access routes, different degrees of sponsoring power, and different scales of monetary worth to the practices in use. An analysis of sponsorship systems of literacy would help educators everywhere to think through the effects that economic and political changes in their regions are having on various people's ability to write and read, their chances to sustain that ability, and their capacities to pass it along to others. Recession, relocation, immigration, technological change, government retreat all can—and do—condition the course by which literate potential develops.

Sponsorship and the Rise in Literacy Standards

As I have been attempting to argue, literacy as a resource becomes available to ordinary people largely through the mediations of more powerful sponsors. These sponsors are engaged in ceaseless processes of positioning and repositioning, seizing and relinquishing control over meanings and materials of literacy as part of their participation in economic and political competition. In the give and take of these struggles, forms of literacy and literacy learning take shape. This section examines more closely how forms of literacy are created out of competitions between institutions. It especially considers how this process relates to the rapid rise in literacy standards since World War II (Resnick and Resnick, 1977). As print and its spinoffs have entered virtually every sphere of life, people have grown increasingly dependent on their literacy skills for earning a living and exercising and protecting their civil rights. This section uses one extended case example to trace the role of institutional sponsorship in raising the literacy stakes. It also considers how one man used available forms of sponsorship to cope with this escalation in literacy demands.

The focus is on Dwayne Lowery, whose transition in the early 1970s from line worker in an automobile manufacturing plant to field representative for a major public employees union exemplified the major transition of the post–World War II economy—from a thing-making, thing-swapping society to an information-making, service-swapping society. In the process, Dwayne Lowery had to learn to read and write in ways that he had never done before. How his experiences with writing developed and how they were sponsored—and distressed—by institutional struggle will unfold in the following narrative.

A man of Eastern European ancestry, Dwayne Lowery was born in 1938, the third of five children of a rubber worker father and a homemaker mother. Lowery recalled how, in his childhood home, his father's feisty union publications and left-leaning newspapers and radio shows helped to create a political climate in his household. "I was sixteen years old before I knew that *goddamn Republicans* was two words," he said. Despite this influence, Lowery said he shunned politics and newspaper reading as a young person, except to read the sports page. A diffident student, he graduated near the bottom of his class from a small high school in 1956 and, after a stint in the Army, went to work on the assembly line of a major automobile manufacturer. In the late 1960s, bored with the repetition of spraying primer paint on fifty-seven cars an hour, Lowery traded in his night shift at the auto plant for a day job reading water meters in a municipal utility department. It was at that time, Lowery recalled, that he rediscovered newspapers, reading them in the early morning in his department's break room. He said:

> At the time I guess I got a little more interested in the state of things within the state. I started to get a little political at that time and got a little more information about local people. So I would buy [a metropolitan paper] and I would read that paper in the morning. It was a pretty conservative paper, but I got some information.

At about the same time Lowery became active in a rapidly growing public employees union, and, in the early 1970s, he applied for and received a union-sponsored grant that allowed him to take off four months of work and travel to Washington, D.C., for training in union activity. Here is his extended account of that experience:

> When I got to school, then there was a lot of reading. I often felt bad. If I had read more [as a high-school student] it wouldn't have been so tough. But they pumped a lot of stuff at us to read. We lived in a hotel, and we had, to some extent, homework we had to do and reading we had to do and not make written reports but make some presentation on our part of it. What they were trying to teach us, I believe, was regulations, systems, laws. In case anything in court came up along the way, we would know that. We did a lot of work on organizing, you know, learning how to negotiate contracts, contractual language, how to write it. Gross National Product, how that affected the Consumer Price Index. It was pretty much a crash course. It was pretty much crammed in. And I'm not sure we were all that well prepared when we got done, but it was interesting.

After a hands-on experience organizing sanitation workers in the West, Lowery returned home and was offered a full-time job as a field staff representative for the union, handling worker grievances and contract negotiations for a large, active local near his state capital. His initial writing and rhetorical activities corresponded with the heady days of the early 1970s, when the union was growing in strength and influence, reflecting in part the exponential expansion in information workers and service providers within all branches of government. With practice, Lowery said he became "good at talking," "good at presenting the union side," "good at slicing chunks off the employer's case." Lowery observed that, in those years, the elected officials with whom he was negotiating often lacked the sophistication of their Washington-trained union counterparts. "They were part-time people," he said. "And they didn't know how to calculate. We got things in contracts that didn't cost them much at the time, but were going to cost them a ton down the road." In time, though, even small municipal and county governments responded to the public employees' growing power by hiring specialized attorneys to represent them in grievance and contract negotiations. "Pretty soon," Lowery observed, "ninety percent of the people I was dealing with across the table were attorneys."

This move brought dramatic changes in the writing practices of union reps, and, in Lowery's estimation, a simultaneous waning of the power of workers and the power of his own literacy. "It used to be we got our way through muscle or through political connections," he said. "Now we had to get it through legalistic stuff. It was no longer just sit down and talk about it. Can we make a deal?" Instead, all activity became rendered in writing: the exhibit, the brief, the transcript, the letter, the appeal. Because briefs took longer to write, the wheels of justice took longer to turn. Delays in grievance hearings became routine, as lawyers and union reps alike asked hearing judges for extensions on their briefs. Things went, in Lowery's words, "from quick, competent justice to expensive and long-term justice."

In the meantime, Lowery began spending up to seventy hours a week at work, sweating over the writing of briefs, which are typically fifteen- to thirty-page documents laying out precedents, arguments, and evidence for a grievant's case. These documents were being forced by the new political economy in which Lowery's union was operating. He explained:

> When employers were represented by an attorney, you were going to have a written brief because the attorney needs to get paid. Well, what do you think, if you were a union grievant and the attorney says, well, I'm going to write a brief and Dwayne Lowery says, well, I'm not going to. Does the worker somehow feel that their representation is less now?

To keep up with the new demands, Lowery occasionally traveled to major cities for two- or three-day union-sponsored workshops on arbitration, new legislation, and communication skills. He also took short courses at a historic School for Workers at a nearby university. His writing instruction consisted mainly of reading the briefs of other field reps, especially those written by the college graduates who increasingly were being assigned to his district from union headquarters. Lowery said he kept a file drawer filled with other people's briefs from which he would borrow formats and phrasings. At the time of our interview in 1995, Dwayne Lowery had just taken an early and somewhat bitter retirement from the union, replaced by a recent graduate from a master's degree program in industrial relations.

Over a twenty-year period, Lowery's adult writing took its character from a particular juncture in labor relations, when even small units of government began wielding (and, as a consequence, began spreading) a "legalistic" form of literacy in order to restore political dominance over public workers. This struggle for dominance shaped the kinds of literacy skills required of Lowery, the kinds of genres he learned and used, and the kinds of literate identity he developed.

Lowery's rank-and-file experience and his talent for representing that experience around a bargaining table became increasingly peripheral to his ability to prepare documents that could compete in kind with those written by his formally educated, professional adversaries. Face-to-face meetings became occasions mostly for a ritualistic exchange of texts, as arbitrators generally deferred decisions, reaching them in private, after solitary deliberation over complex sets of documents. What Dwayne Lowery was up against as a working adult in the second half of the twentieth century was more than just living through a rising standard in literacy expectations or a generalized growth in professionalization, specialization, or documentary power—although certainly all of those things are, generically, true. Rather, these developments should be seen more specifically, as outcomes of ongoing transformations in the history of literacy as it has been wielded as part of economic and political conflict. These transformations become the arenas in which new standards of literacy develop. And for Dwayne Lowery—as well as many like him over the last twenty-five years—these are the arenas in which the worth of existing literacy skills becomes degraded. A consummate debater and deal maker, Lowery saw his value to the union bureaucracy subside, as power shifted to younger, university-trained staffers whose literacy credentials better matched the specialized forms of escalating pressure coming from the other side.

In the broadest sense, the sponsorship of Dwayne Lowery's literacy experiences lies deep within the historical conditions of industrial relations in the twentieth century and, more particularly, within the changing nature of work and labor struggle in what Stevens calls our "advanced contractarian society" (1987, p. 25). For labor, these conditions only intensified in the 1960s and 1970s when a flurry of federal and state civil rights legislation curtailed the previously unregulated hiring and firing power of management. These developments made the appeal to law as central as collective bargaining for extending employee rights (Heckscher, 1988, p. 9). In fact, a history of unionism serves as a guide for a closer look at the sponsors of Lowery's literacy. These resources begin with the influence of his father, whose membership in the United Rubber Workers grounded Lowery in class-conscious progressivism and its favorite literate form: the newspaper. On top of that, though, was a pragmatic philosophy of worker education that developed in the United States, refocusing worker education away from an earlier emphasis on broad critical study and toward discrete techniques for organizing and bargaining. Workers began to be trained in the discrete bodies of knowledge, written formats, and idioms associated with those strategies. Characteristic of this legacy, Lowery's crash course at the Washington-based training center in the early 1970s emphasized technical information, problem solving, and union-building skills and methods. The transformation in worker education from critical, humanistic study to problem-solving skills was also lived out at the School for Workers where Lowery took short courses in the 1980s. Once a place where factory workers came to write and read about economics, sociology, and labor history, the school is now part of a university extension service offering workshops—often requested by management—on such topics as work restructuring, new technology, health and safety regulations, and joint labor-management cooperation. Finally, to this inventory of Dwayne Lowery's literacy sponsors, we must add the latest incarnations shaping union practices: the attorneys and college-educated coworkers who carried into Lowery's workplace forms of legal discourse and what Farr calls "essayist literacy."

What should we notice about this pattern of sponsorship? First, we can see from yet another angle how the course of an ordinary person's literacy learning—its occasions, materials, applications, potentials—follows the transformations going on within sponsoring institutions as those institutions fight for economic and ideological position. As a result of wins, losses, or compromises, institutions undergo change, affecting the kinds of literacy they promulgate and the status that such literacy has in the larger society. So where, how, why, and what Lowery practiced as a writer—and what he didn't practice—took shape as part of the post-industrial jockeying going on over the last thirty years by labor, government, and industry. Yet there is more to be seen in this inventory of literacy sponsors. It exposes the deeply textured history that lies within the literacy practices of institutions and within any individual's literacy experiences. Accumulated layers of sponsoring influences—in families, workplaces, schools, memory—carry forms of literacy that have been shaped out of the ideological and economic struggles of the past. This history, on the one hand, is a sustaining resource in the quest for literacy. It enables an older generation to pass its literacy resources onto another. Lowery's exposure to his father's newspaper reading and supper-table political talk kindled his adult passion for news, debate, and for language that rendered relief and justice. This history also helps to create infrastructures of opportunity. Lowery found crucial supports for extending his adult literacy in the educational networks that unions established during the first half of the twentieth century as they were consolidating into national powers. On the other hand, this layered history of sponsorship is also deeply conservative and can be maladaptive because it teaches forms of literacy that oftentimes are in the process of being overtaken by new political realities and by ascendant forms of literacy. The decision to focus worker education on practical strategies of recruiting and bargaining—devised in the thick of Cold War patriotism and galloping expansion in union memberships—became, by the Reagan years, a fertile ground for new forms of management aggression and cooptation. It is actually this lag or gap in sponsoring forms that we call the rising standard of literacy.

The pace of change and the place of literacy in economic competition have both intensified enormously in the last half of the twentieth century. It is as if the history of literacy is in fast forward. Where once the same sponsoring arrangements could maintain value across a generation or more, forms of literacy and their sponsors can now rise and recede many times within a single life span. Dwayne Lowery experienced profound changes in forms of union-based literacy not only between his father's time and his, but between the time he joined the union and the time he left it, twenty-odd years later. This phenomenon is what makes today's literacy feel so advanced and, at the same time, so destabilized.

Sponsorship and Appropriation in Literacy Learning

We have seen how literacy sponsors affect literacy learning in two powerful ways. They help to organize and administer stratified systems of opportunity and access, and they raise the literacy stakes in struggles for competitive advantage. Sponsors enable and hinder literacy activity, often forcing the formation of new literacy requirements while decertifying older ones. A somewhat different dynamic of literacy sponsorship is treated here. It pertains to the potential of the sponsored to divert sponsors' resources toward ulterior projects, often projects of self-interest or self-development. Earlier I mentioned how Sunday school parishioners in England and African Americans in slavery appropriated church-sponsored literacy for economic and psychic survival. "Misappropriation" is always possible at the scene of literacy transmission, a reason for the tight ideological control that usually surrounds reading and writing instruction. The account that follows is meant to shed light on the dynamics of appropriation, including the role of sponsoring agents in that process. It is also meant to suggest that diversionary tactics in literacy learning may be invited now by the sheer proliferation of literacy activity in contemporary life. The uses and networks of literacy crisscross through many domains, exposing people to multiple, often amalgamated sources of sponsoring powers—secular, religious, bureaucratic, commercial, technological. In other words, what is so destabilized about contemporary literacy today also makes it so available and potentially innovative, ripe for picking, one might say, for people suitably positioned. The rising level of schooling in the general population is also an inviting factor in this process. Almost everyone now has some sort of contact, for instance, with college-educated people, whose movements through workplaces, justice systems, social-service organizations, houses of worship, local government, extended families, or circles of friends spread dominant forms of literacy (whether wanted or not, helpful or not) into public and private spheres. Another condition favorable for appropriation is the deep hybridity of literacy practices extant in many settings. As we saw in Dwayne Lowery's case, workplaces, schools, and families bring together multiple strands of the history of literacy in complex and influential forms. We need models of literacy that more astutely account for these kinds of multiple contacts, both in and out of school and across a lifetime. Such models could begin to grasp the significance of reappropriation, which, for a number of reasons, is becoming a key requirement for literacy learning at the end of the twentieth century.

The following case involves such literacy diversion as it occurred in the life of a secretary who worked for a better-educated male supervisor who taught her reading and writing as a way to perform clerical duties. However, strong loyalties outside the workplace prompted this secretary to lift these literacy resources for use in other spheres. Carol White, an American Indian of the Oneida Nation, was born into a low-income, single-parent household in 1940. She graduated from high school in 1960 and, between five maternity leaves and a divorce, worked continuously in a series of clerical positions in both the private and public sectors. One of her first secretarial jobs was with an urban firm that produced and disseminated Catholic missionary films. The vice president with whom she worked most closely also spent much of his time producing a magazine for a national civic organization that he headed. She discussed how typing letters and magazine articles and occasionally proofreading for this man taught her rhetorical strategies in which she was keenly interested. She described the scene of transfer this way:

> [My boss] didn't just write to write. He wrote in a way to make his letters appealing. I would have to write what he was writing in this magazine too. I was completely enthralled. He would write about the people who were in this [organization] and the different works they were undertaking and people that died and people who were sick and about their personalities. And he wrote little anecdotes. Once in a while I made some suggestions too. He was a man who would listen to you.

The appealing and persuasive power of the anecdote became especially important to Carol White when she began doing door-to-door missionary work for the Jehovah's Witnesses, a pan-racial, millennialist religious faith. She now uses colorful anecdotes to prepare demonstrations that she performs with other women at weekly service meetings at their Kingdom Hall. These demonstrations, done in front of the congregation, take the form of skits designed to explore daily problems through Bible principles. Further, at the time of our interview, Carol White was working as a municipal revenue clerk and had recently enrolled in an on-the-job training seminar called "Persuasive Communication," a two-day class offered free to public employees. Her motivation for taking the course stemmed from her desire to improve her evangelical work. She said she wanted to continue to develop speaking and writing skills that would be "appealing," "motivating," and "encouraging" to people she hoped to convert.

The dynamics of sponsorship alive in this narrative expose important elements of literacy appropriation, at least as it was practiced at the end of the twentieth century. In a pattern now familiar from the earlier sections, we see how opportunities for literacy learning—this time for diversions of resources—open up in the clash between long-standing, residual forms of sponsorship and the new: between the lingering presence of literacy's conservative history and its pressure for change. So, here a secretary filches public relations techniques from a more educated, higher-status man through an ulterior identity with her evangelical faith—one of the earliest avenues by which women (including Native American women) were allowed to pursue literacy. This role, sanctioned deeply within arrangements of an original mass literacy and fused with the more newly permissible activity of feminine clerical work, became grounds for covert, innovative appropriation even as it reinforced a traditional female identity.

Just as multiple identities contribute to the ideologically hybrid character of literacy formations, so do institutional and material conditions. Carol White's account speaks to such hybridity. The missionary film company with the civic club vice president is a residual site for two of literacy's oldest campaigns—Christian conversion and civic participation—enhanced here by twentieth-century advances in film and public relations techniques. This ideological reservoir proved a pleasing instructional site for Carol White, whose interests in literacy, throughout her life, have been primarily spiritual. So literacy appropriation draws upon, perhaps even depends upon, conservative forces in the history of literacy sponsorship that are always hovering at the scene of acts of learning. This history serves as both a sanctioning force and a reserve of ideological and material support. At the same time, individual acts of appropriation can divert and subvert the course of literacy's history and show how changes in individual literacy experience relate to larger-scale transformations. Carol White's redirection of personnel management techniques to the cause of the Jehovah's Witnesses is an almost ironic transformation in this regard. Once a principal sponsor in the initial spread of mass literacy, evangelism is here rejuvenated through late-literate corporate sciences of secular persuasion, fund-raising, and bureaucratic management circulating in Carol White's workplace.

Teaching and the Dynamics of Sponsorship

This chapter has offered a few working case studies that link patterns of sponsorship to processes of stratification, competition, and reappropriation. How much these dynamics can be generalized to classrooms is an ongoing empirical question. I am sure that sponsors play even more influential roles at the scenes of literacy learning and use than this chapter has explored. I have focused on some of the most tangible aspects—material supply, explicit teaching, institutional aegis. But the ideological pressure of sponsors affects many private aspects of writing processes as well as public aspects of finished texts. Where one's sponsors are multiple or even at odds, they can make writing maddening. Where they are absent, they make writing unlikely. Many of the cultural formations we associate with writing development—community practices, disciplinary traditions, technological potentials—can be appreciated as make-do responses to the economics of literacy, past and present. The history of literacy is a catalogue of obligatory relations. That this catalogue is so deeply conservative and, at the same time, so ruthlessly demanding of change is what fills contemporary literacy learning and teaching with their most paradoxical choices and outcomes (for a similar point, see Cremin, 1990).

In bringing attention to economies of literacy learning, I am not advocating that we prepare students more efficiently for the job markets they must enter. What I have tried to suggest is that as we assist and study individuals in pursuit of literacy, we also recognize how literacy is in pursuit of them. When this process stirs ambivalence, on their part or on ours, we need to be understanding.

Notes

1. For a positive treatment of sponsors, see Goldblatt (1994), who explored the power of institutions to authorize writers.
2. My debt to the writings of Pierre Bourdieu will be evident throughout this chapter. Here and throughout I invoke his expansive notion of "economy," which is not restricted to literal and ostensible systems of money making but to the many spheres where people labor, invest, and exploit energies—their own and others'—to maximize advantage. See Bourdieu and Wacquant (1992, especially pp. 117–120), and Bourdieu (1990, Chapter 7).
3. All names used in the chapter are pseudonyms.

References

Applebee, Arthur N., Langer, Judith A., and Mullis, Ida V. S. *The Writing Report Card: Writing Achievement in American Schools*. Princeton, N.J.: Educational Testing Service, 1986.

Bourdieu, Pierre. *The Logic of Practice*. (Richard Nice, trans.) Cambridge, U.K.: Polity, 1990.

Bourdieu, Pierre, and Wacquant, L.J.D. *An Invitation to Reflexive Sociology*. Chicago: Chicago University Press, 1992.

Bourne, J. M. *Patronage and Society in Nineteenth-Century England*. London, U.K.: Edward Arnold, 1986.

Brandt, Deborah. "Accumulating Literacy: Writing and Learning to Write in the 20th Century." *College English*, 1995, *57*, 649–668.

Brandt, Deborah. "Remembering Reading, Remembering Writing." *College Composition and Communication*, 1994, *45*, 459–479.

Cornelius, Janet Duitsman. *"When I Can Ready My Title Clear": Literacy, Slavery, and Religion in the Antebellum South*. Columbia: University of South Carolina, 1991.

Cremin, Lawrence. "The Cacophony of Teaching." In Lawrence A. Cremin (ed.), *Popular Education and Its Discontents*. New York: Harper, 1990.

Faigley, Lester. "Veterans' Stories on the Porch." In Beth Boehm, Debra Journet, and Mary Rosner (eds.), *History, Reflection and Narrative: The Professionalization of Composition, 1963–1983*. Norwood, N.J.: Ablex, 1999.

Farr, Marcia. "Essayist Literacy and Other Verbal Performances." *Written Communication*, 1993, *8*, 4–38.

Goldblatt, Eli. *"Round My Way": Authority and Double Consciousness in Three Urban High-School Writers*. Pittsburgh, Pa.: University of Pittsburgh Press, 1994.

Heckscher, Charles C. *The New Unionism: Employee Involvement in the Changing Corporation*. New York: Basic Books, 1988.

Hortsman, Connie, and Kurtz, Donald V. *Compradrazgo in Post-Conquest Middle America*. Milwaukee: University of Wisconsin-Milwaukee, Center for Latin America, 1978.

Kett, Joseph F. *The Pursuit of Knowledge Under Difficulties: From Self Improvement to Adult Education in America 1750–1990.* Stanford, CA: Stanford University Press, 1994.

Laqueur, Thomas. *Religion and Respectability: Sunday Schools and Working Class Culture 1780–1850.* New Haven: Yale University Press, 1976.

Lynch, Joseph H. *Godparents and Kinship in Early Medieval Europe.* Princeton, N.J.: Princeton University Press, 1986.

Miller, S. *Textual Carnivals: The Politics of Composition.* Carbondale: Southern Illinois University Press, 1991.

Nicholas, Stephen J., and Nicholas, Jacqueline M. "Male Literacy, 'Deskilling,' and the Industrial Revolution." *Journal of Interdisciplinary History,* 1992, *23,* 1–18.

Resnick, Daniel P., and Resnick, Lauren B. "The Nature of Literacy: A Historical Explanation." *Harvard Educational Review,* 1977, *47,* 370–385.

Spellmeyer, Kurt. "After Theory: From Textuality to Attunement with the World." *College English,* 1996, *58,* 893–913.

Stevens, Jr., Edward. *Literacy, Law, and Social Order.* DeKalb: Northern Illinois University Press, 1987.

2

Literacy in American Lives

Living and Learning in a Sea of Change

FOR THE PAST SEVERAL YEARS I HAVE BEEN USING LIFE HISTORY RESEARCH to understand the changing standards for literacy achievement in the United States and elsewhere—the expectation for more and more people to do more and more things with reading and writing (Brandt, 2001). We all can sense these shifting standards in our schools and our societies. We can hear them in pronouncements from politicians, from blue ribbon panels, from disgruntled employers. We can see them in the high-stakes testing movement and other accountability movements. And we can fear them in the tightening association between literacy and viability, both economic and political. In an information economy, literacy or, more broadly, symbol skill is a kind of raw material. It is becoming directly implicated in matters of productivity and economic growth (Boisot, 1999; Drucker, 1998; Stewart, 1997). More and more people are expected to know how to labor with written symbols as our tools. Many of us are expected to produce written symbols as our products. And when we are not working, we are encouraged to traffic in written symbols as part of leisure life. A lot of fortunes are riding on the literacy skills of ordinary people, and that is why we live in a time of great pressure on literacy and on the teachers and learners of literacy.

My research attempts to get behind the blue ribbon pronounce-ments and debates over schooling and instructional methods in order to understand this pressure as it has arisen in the ordinary lives of people in my community. What does it mean to acquire literacy at a time where there is so much at stake around it? How do rapidly chang-ing standards for literacy appear as part of felt life within the experi-ences of individuals, families, or communities? How do people cope with and adapt to these changes? What are the implications for us all?

In the early- and mid-1990s, I interviewed eighty people from all walks of life, collecting their recollections of how they learned to read and write across their lifetimes. The people I talked with ranged in age from ninety-nine to ten. They were all living at the time of the interviews in and around Dane County, Wisconsin, where I live and work. But they had been raised in diverse regions of the United States, including African American sharecropping communities of the South, a Jewish garment-working community in New York City, Mexican American migrant communities of south Texas, a professional com-munity in Silicon Valley, and rural communities throughout the upper Midwest. They were also diverse in terms of education, occupa-tion, religion, language heritage, and reason for being in Dane County, Wisconsin. I interviewed people primarily in their homes. The inter-views lasted anywhere from one hour to three hours. In the interviews, we explored how they learned to read and write, the uses they made of reading and writing at various stages of their lives, and the mean-ing that literacy had for them. In the interviews, we tried to focus on a chronology of memories, beginning as early as we could and proceed-ing through the present. Whenever people had a significant memory, we probed it as deeply as we could. I asked them to remember where the learning took place, who was there, what was there in terms of materials, and what was motivating the learning. These accounts not only shed light on a lot of learning that was taking place outside of school, but also, to an extent I did not foresee, gave me ways of seeing the impacts of literacy across someone's entire lifetime and across and between generations. I also realized, mostly in retrospect, how much regional history I was capturing by studying people in one place, the people who were born there or were drawn there over time. During the course of the twentieth century, Dane County, Wisconsin was transformed—like many places were—from an overwhelmingly agrarian society into a high-tech service society, and the life accounts provided a record of how literacy learning functioned as part of that process.

One of the most striking characteristics of the interviews was that they were filled with references to other people: teachers, relatives, friends, religious figures, military officers, librarians, supervisors, salespeople, therapists, radio voices, favored authors, figures with a powerful presence and often a powerful interest in the outcomes of writing or learning. I spent a long time analyzing these references not only to particular people but to other entities—the Job Corps, the Palmer Method, the Etch-O-Sketch, the Signal Corps, Future Problem Solvers Inc., Sunday school cards, on and on—presences that I came to think of as the sponsors of literacy. I defined sponsors of literacy as those agents, local or distant, concrete or abstract, who teach, model, support, recruit, extort, deny, or suppress literacy and gain advantage by it in some way (Brandt, 1998). Sponsors became the tangible link between individual scenes of writing and reading and larger social, economic, and historical powers of literacy.

The idea of sponsorship resonated for me because it seemed to lie deeply in the history of literacy itself. Patronage is central to the history of publishing, and we know that authors like other artists often depended upon wealthy patrons to support them while they worked. Manuscript culture was kept alive through the patronage of the church. Early booksellers in England and the United States often depended on patrons to advance the capital they needed to publish (Bourne, 1986; Graff, 1986). Many poets and novelists in these times are supported by creative writing programs in colleges and universities. In the history of mass literacy, the story seemed the same— for instance, in the nineteenth century, workers in England or African Americans in slavery found opportunities for literacy learning through the aegis of Protestant churches that wanted to expand their ranks and did so through the teaching of reading (Cornelius, 1991; Laqueur, 1976). In my current research, I am documenting the role of the modern workplace as an engine of literacy instruction and subsidy (Brandt, 2005). Sponsorship also seemed especially appropriate for experience in the twentieth century because the interviews were filled with references to commercial interests—media, toys, games, and later, computer brands—all kinds of commercial sponsors who recruited buyers to and through literacy. Sponsorship also seemed to address the ambivalence that marked many experiences with literacy that were coming out of the interviews. People I talked to generally learned to read and write or learned to work computers or learned to make other adjustments in their communication habits, but they didn't always want to. They had to. Ambivalence is at the heart of the patron-client relationship. Patrons loan what they have—land, money, protection, reputation, favors, access—in order to extend their power or influence. Clients on their side trade labor or deference for access to opportunities for themselves or their families or other kinds of leverage that improves their social standing (Hortsman and Kurtz, 1978). Literacy sponsorship seems to operate like that. Sponsorship creates access and opportunity to something valuable at the same time that it creates obligation and pressure. So the idea of sponsorship seems able to account both for the value that literacy has for individual learners and the value that literate individuals have (and increasingly have) in wider arenas into which their skills are being recruited.

So the analysis brought me to see that literacy and literacy learning are organized by sponsors whose interests are alive and at work at the scenes of our writing and learning. Sponsors affect access to writing and reading. They provide the materials and auspices and often the rationales under which literacy is learned and practiced. As sponsors compete with each other for dominance, they often use literacy as the grounds of competition as they try to gain the upper hand. As a result, the sponsored can find the worth or reach of their literacy skills caught up in inflationary or deflationary spirals. Changing sponsors can destabilize literacy, and what we feel as the changing standards for literacy achievement reflect the fierce economic and political competitions in which literacy, especially now, gets caught up. Sponsors also carry with them beliefs about what literacy is, what it is used for, and where and how it finds value. A sponsor's beliefs often rub off on learners, but whether they actually do or not, changing forms of sponsorship under which people learn to read and write ultimately change the logics and meanings of literacy as a social resource, affecting the political and educational climates in which we teach and learn.

I would like to make these ideas more concrete and more consequential by telling you the stories of two people whom I interviewed and who are featured in the first chapter of *Literacy in American Lives*. I call them Martha Day and Barbara Hunt, and I was drawn to a treatment of these two lives together because they had such fascinating things in common with each other and one dramatic difference.

By her early twenties, Martha Day was a practicing journalist with a farm magazine called *The Mid-Plains Farmer*. Barbara Hunt, in her early twenties, was cashiering at the Mid-Plains Mobil Station, doing child care on the side, and taking an occasional course in the human services program at a two-year technical college twenty-five miles from her home.

The contrast in their birth dates and the work they were doing after high school speaks directly of course to the rising standard for literacy and school achievement across a sixty-year span (Resnick and Resnick, 1977). Martha Day's high school graduation in 1920 made her among the best-educated members of her community, while the only thing guaranteed to high school graduates by the 1990s was that

MARTHA DAY AND BARBARA HUNT

Both developed identities as writers early in their lives and aspired to careers that would involve them in writing.

- Both liked to read for pleasure.
- Both kept journals.
- Both used writing in extracurricular activities in school (yearbook, forensics).
- Both were the middle of three children.
- Both were reared on eighty-acre, low-income dairy farms inherited by their parents.
- Both grew up in sparsely populated rural settlements some distance from schools and stores.
- Neither had money or familial encouragement for schooling beyond the twelfth grade.
- Both left home and went to work shortly after high school graduation.
- Martha Day was born in 1904.
- Barbara Hunt was born in 1971.

they were likely to earn several hundred thousand dollars less over their lifetimes than college graduates. But there is more to it than this. Martha Day came of age when the small, family-farm economy in the Midwest was worth more, literally in terms of dollars and jobs and also culturally and socially. At the beginning of the twentieth century, Martha Day belonged to the 40 percent of the U.S. population engaged in the agricultural sector. By the time of Barbara Hunt's birth in 1971, farm kids belonged to the 2 percent of the population still in agriculture. Martha Day's residence on an eighty-acre farm and her attendance at a two-room country school made her background typical of European Americans in her predominantly rural state. Sixty years later, rural schools had joined urban schools in being chronically underfinanced in comparison with suburban districts, and family-owned dairy farms were disappearing from the Wisconsin landscape at a rate of a thousand farms a year (Census of Agriculture, 1992). What did these differences have to do with the literacy experiences of these two women? (In other words, how do the factors in the second half of the list matter to the first half of the list?)

Martha Day's childhood coincided with the "golden age of agriculture," a twenty-year period at the turn of the century when average farm incomes were doubling, the value of farmland was more than tripling, and profits and tax revenues were invested in local improvements (Danborn, 1995). Many of Martha Day's earliest literacy memories are linked to innovations that were making life better: electric lights, paved roads, rural mail delivery, farm journalism, and expanding schooling that developed as part of an unprecedented boom time in Midwestern rural areas (Nelson, 1995). Like many people I interviewed who were children during this period, Martha Day proudly recalled a progressive family identity that seemed to be delivered into many rural households along with the local newspaper. Periodical reading was linked to forward-looking thinking, intelligent farming, and political participation. Here is a memory of her father, who had left school in the eighth grade:

> Dad always subscribed to [the nearest daily] and took it by the year. My Dad was smart and a good scholar and a most interested man in politics and everything that was going on. I don't remember reading it much, but I remember when my father came in from working in the fields, the first thing he'd do was, if the mail had come, he would sit down and read the newspaper. He was very sharp on that kind of thing. For that day.

Martha Day attended grade school in one of the many two-story brick schoolhouses in what she called "the typical little village of that day." There was "a school, a church, and a general store." They were all located within a mile of the family farm, and they were led or owned by members of the local community—people known to Martha Day and people who knew each other. In school Martha Day developed "a love of writing" that was encouraged by her mother and was often used as part of her play with her siblings. A good student, she continued on to high school along with her brother, commuting ten miles to the nearest large town for her studies. At the age of eighty-nine, Martha Day was still stinging from what she considered the gender discrimination that sent her brother away to college while she stayed in the area to care for her invalid mother. "[My brother's] teachers encouraged him," she explained. "They got a rector scholarship. Told him about it. Nobody told me. I made grades just as good as his. But they didn't push girls, and my parents couldn't have sent us on." Instead, in 1921, when her mother was well enough, Martha Day moved fifty miles to Indianapolis, worked in the book department of a large department store and took secretarial courses at night.

Martha Day was part of a major migration of the 1920s—an outflow of young people from the country to the city (Danborn, 1995). She became an early information worker, caught up in the growth of a service economy dependent on relatively high levels of literacy that high schools were creating. Still the social network from the farm community carried over into life in the city. There family connections continued to matter as she made the transition to nonfarm work. "I never did have to hunt for jobs," she said of this period of her life. "Somebody from my area always said, 'Call me' or 'We've got a job. Would you be interested in it?' I had a job with the tax commissioners and then, while I was on that job, somebody called me that knew my family and asked if I would be interested in a job as secretary to the vice president of an insurance company." These social networks were informal and overlapping, and soon they helped her make her break into journalism. After she married a bookkeeper in 1925, Martha Day and her husband began attending a Methodist Sunday school class for young married couples that was taught by the managing editor of a local newspaper. Aware of Martha Day's interest in writing, he asked her to put together a monthly newsletter for the Sunday school group. Two years later, this man bought a small, regional farm magazine and invited Martha Day to become a part-time "rewrite man," as she called herself. Her job was to recast into short news items the press releases and bulletins that were pouring out of the state agricultural university and experimental stations at that time.

Martha Day worked at home, with a typewriter, desk, and filing cabinet that the editor provided. Each Sunday, she brought her rewrites to church and received a new batch of assignments. Occasionally, the editor asked her to write a feature story, usually about a farm woman. The editor was instrumental in teaching Martha Day classic elements of journalistic style.

> He kept building me up, you know, giving me a little more instruction. How the first paragraph had to do this and so forth. He would try to coach me along. He'd say, "Imagine you are a farm woman." That I grew up on a farm helped me in some respects. It wouldn't today.

This figure of the editor is quite interesting to me because he carries in his influence both the role of the church and the role of the press in spreading mass literacy. They are here embodied literally in the same person, in the same sponsor. But this figure also became an agent of change. By the 1940s, commercial farm publishing was flourishing (Evans and Salcedo, 1974). The newspaper man's local farm journal was bought out by a much larger conglomerate, the *Mid-Plains Farmer*. Martha Day was invited to move to corporate offices and, throughout several more buyouts and mergers, gradually assumed more editorial responsibility. She contributed a bimonthly column on domestic topics, compiled cookbooks that were distributed as complimentary promotions, and traveled regularly to Chicago and other big cities for editorial meetings or conventions. She retired in 1968. At the time of our interview she was widowed and residing near her daughter in a residential care facility in Wisconsin, some three hundred miles from her birthplace. She wrote letters to church friends, some from the original adult Sunday school class, and showed me extensive memoirs she had written in several bound journals that her daughter had bought for her. Although her eyesight was deteriorating, she had recently composed a humorous poem about osteoporosis that a nurse helped her to get published in a health magazine for senior citizens.

Martha Day's account illustrates two important connections among economics, sponsorship, and literacy. First, we can see how the cultural and social organization of a particular economy creates reservoirs of opportunity and constraint from which individuals take their literacy, and, second, how these backgrounds can later become exploited by agents of change. Martha Day's memories of early literacy learning carry the tensions that were alive in rural, white societies at the turn of the century, as conservative values of farm and village shaped young people, even while they were heading for lives elsewhere. For Martha Day, these tensions registered most painfully for her in gender inequality. While both she and her brother left the farm, he went to college and to an eventual science career in the nation's capital. She took her interest in reading and writing fifty miles to her state capital for jobs selling books and taking dictation. Yet staying back left her tethered to the conservative social institutions out of which her subsequent literacy opportunities would come—as would the exploitable value of that experience. This legacy provided the point of contact for Martha Day's entrance into paid, professional writing and sanctioned the informal apprenticeship by which she learned her trade. Martha Day's background became an exploitable resource when the farm magazine industry took off in the 1940s. Farm magazines attempted to appeal to the entire farm family, to uphold the agrarian tradition even while they were pushing products and practices that would transform the business of farming (Neth, 1995; Walters, 1996). Women's news was crucial to the commercial success of these magazines. They carried features on topics such as gardening, canning, dress, diet, faith, and marriage. Martha Day wrote on all of these topics in her column, which was often organized around the seasonal rhythms of the farm life she experienced growing up. She wrote, that is, until full-scale national women's magazines like *Ladies Home Journal* and *Good Housekeeping* put her out of a job.

The person of Martha Day, the badge of her integrity in her home community, became a badge of her value to the enterprise of farm journalism as it was being practiced at this time. Her conservative farm background, her Methodist mores, her ideological comfort with print as an agent of improvement all enabled her to voice the values that the *Mid-Plains Farmer* needed for commercial success. These commercial needs became the vehicle for Martha Day's adult literacy development. However, this window of opportunity was brief. By the time Martha Day retired in the late 1960s, general farm magazines were on the wane, women weren't home anymore to be interviewed for her feature stories, more and more of her published recipes came from large food-processing industries, and agribusiness was changing the farm economy from top to bottom. Before these changes, however, Martha Day fulfilled her desire to be a writer, and these opportunities were still immensely satisfying and motivating to her. At the age of eighty-nine, she was still writing and placing an occasional feature story in senior citizens' magazines.

I do not wish to suggest that Martha Day's experience was the only experience of farm people of her generation. Many did not have the same opportunities. However, her case illustrates in its particulars how dynamics of economic competition create the context in which literacy resources can be pursued, expended, enjoyed, and rewarded. For Martha Day, membership in a cultural majority within a stable and, even at times, expanding economy provided both the means and mentality for her literate interests and skills to pay off. While Martha Day made a successful transition from agricultural to intellectual labor, the transition depended on being well connected to an older order upon whose values she could continue to trade.

By the time Barbara Hunt was born in 1971, the golden age of agriculture was long gone. Her father operated a cash-strapped dairy farm during some of the most crisis-ridden years in the history of the dairy industry. Wisconsin saw a 50 percent decline in farms between the 1960s and the 1990s, with the biggest jump between 1987 and 1992, the years that Barbara Hunt was attending high school (Saupe, 1989). In one of the many eerie contrasts between the testimonies of Martha Day and Barbara Hunt, Barbara told me she remembered reading the newspaper at home and seeing her father's budget calculations in pencil in the margins—a statement of the uneasy financial situation they were in and the level of worry and preoccupation that prevailed. Like Martha Day, Barbara Hunt grew up in a small, ethnically homogeneous community founded in the nineteenth century by German Catholic clerics and dairy keepers. At one time it had been one of the main production areas in the state for butter, grain, and tobacco. The community is still anchored by a stone church built in the 1850s, and most of the residents are related to each other. But at the end of the twentieth century, this unincorporated village had no schools and little commercial base left. Barbara Hunt rode a bus ten miles north across the county line for grade school, and her family drove twenty miles south to find a major shopping district.

Barbara Hunt's residence in a village that had grown little in ninety years was not "typical for its day," and its homogeneity was no longer relevant to the structure of labor, as many residents scattered each morning in their cars for service jobs across the county. Farm concerns no longer dominated the regional newspapers to which residents of her community subscribed, and the regional radio, national television networks, and film that infiltrated the Hunt household in the 1970s and 1980s primarily delivered urban-oriented images, information, and perspectives. (Barbara Hunt recalled with a laugh missing her favorite TV sitcoms because of evening milking chores and then having to watch *The Waltons* and *Little House on the Prairie*, which were on at a later hour.) Her school system, answerable to state mandates, typically strained out local culture from its curriculum. Although as a teenager Barbara Hunt was discovering a love of writing and searching for avenues for this drive, she was acquiring literacy as part of a demographic minority. Compared to Martha Day, her literacy sponsors were remote and more difficult to come by. Her paying jobs were not related to agriculture, but rather to low-end retail and government-subsidized services common to areas with stagnant economies. After high school she was hired as a home health aide and charted the weight and pulse of elderly clients on Medicare. But she was laid off when, during major HMO reshuffling in the county, the agency relocated. In the mid 1990s, Barbara Hunt's most steady source of income was in day care and private babysitting, as farm adults sought off-farm employment to stanch the loss of incomes. ("Right now I'm babysitting, and I always read to the kids 'cause I think you should. It sinks in," she said.)

Barbara Hunt did get a chance for meaningful writing because of two connections that are worthy of exploration: one was the Wisconsin High School Forensic Association to which she belonged for five years and the other was the human resources program of a two-year technical college, where she attended part-time. Both of these institutions were in some ways helping Barbara Hunt to develop her literate potential and carry it into her local economy. The Forensic Association is particularly interesting because of its long ties with the Midwest agrarian tradition.

Barbara Hunt joined the forensic club in eighth grade. "As soon as I heard about it, I knew I wanted to be in it," she said. For one thing, being in the club allowed her to satisfy a lifelong quirk: the love of reading aloud. As a member of the forensic club, Barbara Hunt first competed in the category of declamation, reciting published dramatic pieces from memory. But by high school, she was performing in the original speech division, composing and delivering four- and eight-minute speeches.

The forensic club in her high school was part of the oldest state-wide consortium of speech, debate, and theater clubs in the United States (Brockhaus, 1949). In earlier years it was sponsored by the state extension service and on occasion sponsored joint competitions with Future Farmers of America. By the time Barbara Hunt was a member, the Forensic Association had become an independent organization subsidized by dues from member schools. Headquarters provided handbooks and other instructional guides, trained and certified speech coaches, sponsored regional and statewide competitions, and published a newsletter.

As a participant in competitions, Barbara Hunt wrote speeches on topics of her choice. She picked topics that, in her words, "had real emotion," involving issues that "affected me but kind of affected other people." Her preferred topics included abortion, crack use, racism, and homelessness. "I did a lot with homelessness," she explained. "The homeless problem at the time was during my sophomore year, 1986–87. There were three million homeless people in the United States. I wanted to get people to realize what was going on." (I want to think that all that land loss that was going on around Barbara Hunt had something to do with her connection to this topic.)

To write her speeches, she used the school library as well as notes she took from TV news and magazine shows. Song lyrics that she heard on the radio also helped her to reflect on her life and her speech topics. "Songs to me are like some books or some speeches," she said, "when they seem to be exactly what your life is." Barbara Hunt also sometimes enhanced her presentations with film clips taped on a VCR. She practiced her speeches while doing the chores:

> I'd be going along the front of the cows, feeding them with my shovel, and I'd be doing my speech. Dad probably got so sick of me. He never knew what I was saying because I would never tell him what I was actually saying. I would say it to the cows so he never knew what I was practicing. I could probably give my homeless speech right now, though, if I really thought about it.

Barbara Hunt traveled throughout the region with her speech team, qualifying a couple of times for championships held in the state capital. She also found satisfaction when she developed original introductions that were praised by her coach and sometimes imitated by other students.

Despite its many transformations over a one-hundred-year period, the Forensic Association was carrying forward remnants of an oratorical culture that had traditionally sponsored literacy of rural students. The organization subsidized public forums in which Barbara Hunt usually had more freedom to express herself than in school or Sunday school. That her writing could be performed orally was a powerful incentive for her continuous membership in the organization—one of the few to which she belonged in high school. This format also appealed to her ethical sensibilities. "When you give a speech, you have to know the material," she said. "I love it when people [in the competitions] know their speeches and are looking right at you as they give them."

For Barbara Hunt, high school forensics sustained oratorical and ethical values long associated with Midwestern agrarian politics and local self-improvement organizations. Through her speeches, Barbara Hunt was able to articulate issues that, as she said, "affected me but kind of affected other people." Like Martha Day, she was voicing the conditions of her time and place, but translated through urban equivalents that dominated national media as well as the prepackaged research materials in her high school library. The expression of rural social problems through dominant urban ones was not a rhetorical dilemma Martha Day faced as a writer.

At the time of our interview, the writing that Barbara Hunt did for her forensic club was finding some resonance in a psychology class she was taking in the human services program offered at the urban technical college to which she was commuting. In the class, she wrote short essays on contemporary social problems. The course was part of a two-year degree program that had begun in the early 1980s to prepare people as technical assistants in programs such as drug rehabilitation or family counseling. The program responded to a growing regional demand for professionalization in social work, which accompanied increased private and public investments in child and family welfare. According to its director, the program had become a popular vocational choice for young, first-generation college women from rural areas.

Although it is too soon to predict the full life and literacy trajectory of Barbara Hunt, it is clear that many of the local, cultural assets that subsidized Martha Day as she made her way into literacy either are not available to the younger woman or simply are no longer worth as much in her society. The dairy farm life that Barbara Hunt was born to will be hard to parlay directly into economic opportunities—except insofar that it has fine-tuned her sensitivity to human distress. But a sensitivity to her rural time and place needs lots of reinterpretation and transformation to operate in the fields of social service as they were taught and practiced at the end of the twentieth century. To become a writer in her chosen field, Barbara Hunt needs to negotiate formal academic training and complex bureaucracies. Again, these are rhetorical complexities that did not confront Martha Day—at least not so centrally—in her break into journalism.

Literacy learning is conditioned by economic changes and the implications they bring to regions and communities in which students live. Economic changes devalue once-accepted standards of literacy achievement but, more seriously, they destabilize the social and cultural trade routes along which families and communities once learned to preserve and pass on literate know-how. As new and more powerful forms of literacy emerge, they diminish the reach of receding ones. Over the last seventy years, a lopsided competition between corporate agribusiness and family farming altered life for millions of people in the rural United States. The accounts of Martha Day and Barbara Hunt can aid speculation about where in the processes of literacy learning economic changes like this can have the greatest impact. First, we must notice the potential advantages that come with being well connected to dominant economies, whether in periods of stability or change. Dominant economies make their interests visible in social structures and communication systems. Growing up in the heyday of independent agriculture, Martha Day literally could see her way of life reflected everywhere—from the close proximity of the social institutions that sponsored her childhood literacy to the stories and pictures carried in the print media she encountered. Being in the mainstream can enhance literacy development even during periods of stressful transition because at least for a while the powerful resources and skills built up in well-developed economies are attractive sites for reappropriation by agents of change. But as family farming receded in economic and cultural dominance, its social structures weakened as a presence in the world around Barbara Hunt. There was a mismatch between the conditions in which her family lived and labored and the conditions in which she was forced to learn to write and find a living. It is here where economic disadvantage and literacy disadvantage find their relationship.

As investments in local education, commerce, and social welfare drain away from a community, the process damages the institutions by which literacy learning is sponsored. For these reasons, making literacy, like making money, was proving more complicated for Barbara

Hunt than for Martha Day, requiring considerable ingenuity, translation, and adaptation. In her early twenties she was learning to write for an economy she aspired to join while enjoying few of the powerful subsidies that the sponsors of that economy contribute to literacy learning. This is a condition faced by millions of literacy learners of all ages at the start of the twenty-first century, whose ways of life and labor are undergoing permanent destruction and replacement. While they are often painted with the brush of low literacy skills or failure to adapt, we can see in this case of Barbara Hunt that low literacy is not always and, in my view, not usually the problem: rather it is the lack of subsidy for literate potential that is especially crucial in periods of change.

I have tried to get beyond the rhetoric that usually surrounds literacy and the economic needs of a nation. Economic changes create immediate needs for students to cope with gradual and sometimes dramatic alterations in systems of access and reward for literacy learning that operate beyond the classroom. Downsizing, migrations, welfare cutbacks, commercial development, transportation, and technological innovations do not merely form the background buzz of contemporary life. These changes, where they occur, can wipe out as well as create access to supports for literacy learning. They also can inflate or deflate the value of existing forms of literacy in the lives of students. To animate our work with historical consciousness is to better appreciate the predicament of students positioned in receding economies. To be viable, Barbara Hunt, mostly on her own and in the span of a lifetime, must accomplish an abrupt transition from family farm to twenty-first-century postindustrialism, a transition that took the country as a whole an entire century or more to accomplish. Yet in too many government reports and accountability standards, this transition is simply assumed, taken for granted. It is up to us as teachers, scholars, and citizens to resist this amnesia.

References

Boisot, M. H. *Knowledge Assets: Securing Competitive Advantage in the Information Economy.* New York: Oxford University Press, 1999.

Bourne, J. M. *Patronage and Society in Nineteenth-Century England.* London, U.K.: Edward Arnold, 1986.

Brandt, D. "Sponsors of Literacy." *College Composition and Communication,* 1998, *49,* 165–185.

Brandt, D. *Literacy in American Lives.* New York: Cambridge University Press, 2001.

Brandt, D. Writing for a Living: Literacy and the Knowledge Economy. *Written Communication,* 2005, *22,* 166–197.

Brockhaus, H. H. *The History of the Wisconsin High School Forensic Association.* Unpublished dissertation. University of Wisconsin–Madison, 1949.

Census of Agriculture. Washington, D.C.: Bureau of the Census, 1992.

Cornelius, J. *"When I Can Read My Title Clear": Literacy, Slavery, and Religion in the Antebellum South.* Columbia: University of South Carolina Press, 1991.

Danborn, D. B. *Born in the Country: A History of Rural America.* Baltimore, Md.: Johns Hopkins University Press, 1995.

Drucker, P. F. "From Capitalism to Knowledge Society." In D. Neef (ed.), *The Knowledge Economy.* Boston: Butterworth-Heinemann, 1998, pp. 15–34.

Evans, J. F., and Salcedo, J. F. *Communications in Agriculture: The American Farm Press.* Ames: Iowa State University Press, 1974.

Graff, H. J. *Legacies of Literacy: Continuities and Contradictions in Western Culture and Society.* Bloomington: Indiana University Press, 1986.

Hortsman, C., and Kurtz, D. V. *Compadrazgo in Post-Conquest Middle America.* Milwaukee: University of Wisconsin–Milwaukee, Center for Latin America, 1978.

Laqueur, T. *Religion and Respectability: Sunday Schools and Working Class Culture 1780–1850.* New Haven, Conn.: Yale University Press, 1976.

Nelson, D. *Farm and Factory: Workers in the Midwest, 1880–1990.* Bloomington: Indiana University Press, 1995.

Neth, M. *Preserving the Family Farm: Women, Community and the Foundations of Agribusiness in the Midwest, 1900–1940.* Baltimore, Md.: Johns Hopkins University Press, 1995.

Resnick, D. P., and Resnick, L. B. "The Nature of Literacy: An Historical Explanation." *Harvard Educational Review,* 1977, *47,* 370–385.

Saupe, W. F. *How Family Farms Deal with Unexpected Financial Stress.* University of Wisconsin–Madison: Community Economics Paper Series, 1989.

Stewart, T. A. *Intellectual Capital: The New Wealth of Organizations.* New York: Doubleday, 1997.

Walters, G. "The Ideology of Success in Major American Farm Magazines 1934–1991." *Journalism and Mass Communication Quarterly,* 1996, *71,* 594–608.

3

Accumulating Literacy

Writing and Learning to Write in the Twentieth Century

GENNA MAY WAS BORN IN 1898 ON A SMALL DAIRY FARM IN SOUTH-CENTRAL WISCONSIN, the eighth of nine children of Norwegian immigrants. She spoke no English when she enrolled at the age of seven in a one-room schoolhouse built on land donated to the school district by her parents. Although Genna May would eventually go on to complete high school (as one of a graduating class of thirteen) by boarding in a town ten miles from her farm, she started school at a time when Wisconsin required only that young people ages seven to fifteen attend a local grammar school for twelve weeks a year (Landes and Solomon, 1972, p. 56). As a student in "the grades," as she calls them, Genna May wrote spelling lessons on slates, erasing with a wet cloth to go on to arithmetic lessons. She remembers a home with few books and little paper, and she said she would have had no reason to write as a girl except to compose an occasional story assigned by her teacher. After high school graduation in 1917, she enrolled for several months in a private business college in the state capital, just long enough to learn typing and shorthand and win a certificate in penmanship before being placed by the college in the office of a local business that was manufacturing disinfectants for dairy farms. In 1994, Genna May was using writing to record recipes, balance her checkbook, and send holi-day and birthday greetings to family members.

Genna May's great-grandson Michael May was born in 1981 in a sprawling suburb east of Wisconsin's state capital. In the early 1990s he was attending a middle school equipped with computers. The first of four children in his family, Michael remembered that his earliest com-posing occurred at two years old, when his parents helped him form simple words with magnetic letters on a metal easel and chalkboard in the family's TV room. As a participant in a grade-school enrichment program called Future Problem Solvers, he wrote a letter to his princi-pal arranging to correct erosion on the school playground. In the bed-room of his eight-year-old sister Rhonda was a manual typewriter that their father had bought and used while attending a local technical school, a typewriter that Rhonda was now using recreationally. One weekend Michael's mother brought home a personal computer from her job as a data processor at a national insurance company so that she could learn a new program, and, Michael remembered, she allowed him and his sister to type messages back and forth to each other on it. Asked what made writing important to him, Michael responded that it "has a lot to do with speaking," with "seeing correct words."

These accounts by two members of the same family capture many of the economic and social transformations of twentieth-century America: population movements from farms to urban centers to sub-urbs; shifts in the economic base from agriculture to manufacturing to information processing; the rise of big business; a rapid escalation in educational expectations; revolutions in communication technol-ogy; and the growth of a print culture so saturating that it has become a principal means by which some children learn to talk. Against that backdrop we see the dramatically different social contexts in which Genna May and her great-grandson learned about literacy and its relationship to the world. In the sparse setting of Genna May's prai-rie farmhouse, paper, hard to come by, was reserved for her father's church work. In Michael May's print-cluttered suburban ranch home, his parents introduced him to writing and reading amid the background chatter of network television. For members of the community in which Mrs. May grew up, the ability to write the words of everyday life often marked the end of formal schooling, while for Michael May these same experiences served as a preparation for kindergarten. In the social dynamic of the rural school district of the 1890s, it would not have been unusual for a teacher to board with her students' families while school was in session. Three generations later, in a twenty-five–room middle school, students learned to address their principal by formal letter as a lesson in bureaucratic action.

These accounts complicate the argument that the demand now is simply for more people to achieve a kind of literacy that used to be achieved only by a few or, as Lauren Resnick (1987) has put it, that everyone now has to develop reading and writing skills that used to belong only to an elite. However, to say merely that social changes dictate that Michael May achieve a higher level of literacy and education than his great-grandmother is to miss how the same social changes that demand higher eventual skills are already tangibly present at the scene of his literacy learning, part of the way a two-year-old in the 1980s learned what literacy is. Not even elites of the past have encountered the current contexts in which literacy in its many forms is being practiced and learned.

In fact, these accounts suggest that what is unprecedented about literacy learning (and teaching) in the current climate is not so much a demand for literacy that seems chronically to outstrip supply, but rather the challenges faced by all literacy learners in a society whose rapid changes are themselves tied up so centrally with literacy and its enterprises. If Genna May carved out an early life amid a scarcity of print, her great-grandson must carve one out amid a material and ideological surplus. The setting in which Michael May first encountered the ABCs is layered with discarded and emergent forms of literacy and their histories. With his magnetic slate, he recapitulates in eerie ways a rudimentary ritual of the nineteenth-century schoolhouse at the same time that he must absorb from his parents the meanings that literacy and education have for middle-class families of the late-twentieth century. (See Cochran-Smith, 1984; Heath, 1984, Chap. 7.)

The piling up and extending out of literacy and its technologies give a complex flavor even to elementary acts of reading and writing today. Contemporary literacy learners—across positions of age, gender, race, class, and language heritage—find themselves having to piece together reading and writing experiences from more and more spheres, creating new and hybrid forms of literacy where once there might have been fewer and more circumscribed forms. What we calculate as a rising standard of basic literacy may be more usefully regarded as the effects of a rapid proliferation and diversification of literacy. And literate ability at the end of the twentieth century may be best measured as a person's capacity to amalgamate new reading and writing practices in response to rapid social change.

This argument grows out of my reflections upon a set of interviews I conducted during 1992 and 1993 with sixty-five ordinary Americans. I collected their accounts of their own literacy development. Participants explored with me the institutions, materials, and people they believed were most influential in teaching them to write. We also discussed their motivations for learning to write at different stages of their lives. The sixty-five people were selected to represent a stratified sample of the population according to 1990 U.S. Census Bureau categories of age, region of birth, race and ethnicity, education, and occupation. Interviews typically lasted between one and three hours and normally took place in the participants' homes. To protect identities of participants, I refer to all of them throughout this chapter by pseudonyms.

My aim here is to identify several of the major effects of "accumulating literacy" that are especially pertinent to teachers of writing

and reading who are trying to think more broadly about the historical context in which we are carrying out our work. We might visualize
these effects as developing in two directions—vertically (a piling up)
and horizontally (a spreading out). Literacy "piles up" in the twentieth century, among other ways, in the rising levels of formal schooling
that begin to accumulate (albeit inequitably) in families. It is useful to
consider the impact of rising levels of schooling on the way that new
generations of learners encounter and interpret literacy. Literacy also
"piles up" in the twentieth century in a residual sense, as materials and
practices from earlier times often linger at the scenes of contemporary
literacy learning. As I will explore more fully here, the history of literacy in the United States has involved a series of transformations in the
ideological basis of its practices, transformations that gradually co-opt
and eclipse earlier versions. However, because changes in the twentieth
century have become so much more rapid, the ideological texture of
literacy has become more complex as more layers of earlier forms
of literacy exist simultaneously within the society and within the
experiences of individuals. When Genna May and her great-grandson
exchange written greetings at birthdays and holidays, we can appreciate how the complexity of contemporary life derives in part from the
fact that so many generations of literacy, so to speak, now occupy
the same social space. As will be explored more fully here, this residual
character of literacy can serve as both resource and barrier for learners.

The following sections trace the effects of accumulating literacy
through the contours of individual lives. I will focus on the lives of
two middle-class American men: Sam May (the son of Genna May and
grandfather of Michael), whose birth in 1925 between the two World
Wars placed him between a fading literacy of Midwestern rural gentility and a quickly emerging literacy of industrial technology; and
Jordan Grant, born in 1948, the son of a Southern Christian Methodist
Episcopal (C.M.E.) minister, for whom a legacy of liberatory religious literacy enhanced secular advances during the civil rights era

of the 1960s and beyond. These two extended examples will demonstrate several of the key qualities of twentieth-century literacy learning recounted in the interviews overall, particularly the way individuals transform and amalgamate literacy practices in response to—or as part of—rapid social change. In the end, I will explore the implications for contemporary teachers of reading and writing.

"It Was All Done with Words": Literacy Learning Between the World Wars

To consider what these dynamics of accumulating literacy actually have meant to ordinary Americans, we now rejoin the May family, this time focusing on Sam May, the son of Genna May and grandfather of Michael. At the time of our interview, Sam May was nearing retirement from his position as an electronics technician in a science laboratory in a large state university. Born in 1925 and raised as part of an extended family in his mother's rural homestead among other families of Norwegian immigrants, Sam May attended the same sparsely equipped schoolhouse as his mother through the eighth grade. He also attended the same high school as his mother had (this time making the ten-mile trip by carpool) and graduated in 1942, at a time when graduation rates in American high schools were doubling with each generation (Cremin, 1988, p. 230; also see Resnick, 1991).

At home, Sam May was raised into a literacy of gentility and upward mobility promoted especially by his aunt, an invalid and autodidact, who had left school after the eighth grade yet wrote columns and editorials for a local newspaper. She had taken classes through the Palmer School in Iowa, becoming "famous for her fancy hand," and gave Sam and his two siblings penmanship lessons on rainy Saturday afternoons. "My mother's sister was always chiding us to read better books and practice more writing," he explained.

In many of Sam May's recollections of early literacy learning, one detects still influential associations between language correctness and good breeding so prevalent in nineteenth-century ideologies of the upwardly mobile middle class—a literacy that was also designed to express a local identity and community ethos. Above all, literacy learning was part of acquiring manners. "We had to have manners," Mr. May explained. "If the minister was to be at the table on Sunday, we all were supposed to be able to talk a little bit to anyone who was there, or if someone important was there." Mr. May described the impression made on him by the language habits of older, wealthy people who lived in his village, people for whom he would do occasional yard work:

> I was exposed to some pretty high-class people early in life—people who had thousands of bucks and mansions—and they took me in. They used proper grammar in their talking, their speech, and their actions were geared such that you felt comfortable with them. It all had to do with words. If they wrote a note for you, it was beautiful handwriting, and, gosh, I wish I could have done that. [They] had a cultured way about them which we little farm boys would try to emulate. At the time. I've since given it up!

While early school experiences seemed to reinforce many of these values ("spelling and neatness were very important to the teachers"), other influences pressed in—and were brought in—by new technologies. Sam May recalled frequent writing in connection with outdoor boyhood play, such as leaving messages for his friends on the sides of their forts and developing a "code machine" ("two papers that slid around"), inspired by the decoder rings promoted on the radio show "Little Orphan Annie." He also recalled collaborating with large groups of children on "sideshows" that they wrote and performed in connection with weekly outdoor movie nights that started up in the village during the warm months. The children would charge people a few cents each to watch their skits, which were organized in circuslike or vaudeville fashion yet were also inspired by the celluloid action:

> When I was from the age of ten on, they had weekly outdoor movies. On Thursday night five hundred people would come into this little town, sit down on the grass, and watch a Western. It was put on by the businesses. So it was like carnival night. . . . Well, there weren't any live people up there so [we figured] let's make a sideshow. We had to write these flyers, and we would have to write these scripts, and there had to be a master of ceremonies [who would] have to organize this thing, and maybe even write down what he had to say, at least the order in which the show was going to come off. Then we'd have a little dance and there would be someone singing. It was all fun. It was great.

As Mr. May explained, with the Depression, large families were moving to rural communities like his, where vegetable gardens could be grown and barter was more acceptable. Composing skits, plays, circus routines, and secret messages was a way for children to build and maintain community during this transient time. Collaborative writing developed as a necessity. ("If you had a neighborhood play and there was only one person organizing it all," Mr. May explained, "the rest of the kids would quit!") Yet Mr. May's memories also address in interesting ways how intrusions of the new technologies of film and radio stimulated writing and altered recreational literacy.

For example, the converging of farm families to watch Westerns on Thursday nights created a new, public audience beyond family or school for whom Sam May and his playmates could perform, as well as new visual genres to fuel their imaginations. The film nights also created an economic niche in which children could write and perform for money. New technology stimulated writing in other ways too. Radio shows such as "Little Orphan Annie" and "Jack Armstrong" encouraged Sam May and his siblings to write letters to distant radio stations to acquire decoder rings. And the radio became an additional forum for communicating standards of correct or finer speech—a matter that continued to draw Mr. May's attention:

> So to listen to those stories of "The Shadow" or "Orson Welles Theatre" or "Mercury Theatre." God, you could get right in. I mean, you could picture this whole thing going on and it was all done with words. In our neighborhood plays we would try to reconstruct that or if you were entertaining some relatives or a friend. Or if you got a little poem that your mother wants you to read in front of them, a dozen relatives, because they think it's good and you want to show off. And you read this dumb thing and you realize how really limited you are compared to Orson Welles. You were always comparing yourself to Orson Welles.

We can gauge in Mr. May's recollections a more complicated, even contradictory literacy landscape in comparison to what his mother remembered. In a period of rapidly rising educational expectations and painful economic dislocations, Sam May was still being oriented to a legacy of nineteenth-century rural literacy practices based on oral performance, piety, manners, and communal expression—a legacy transmitted principally through the self-education of a member of the previous generation. This legacy in turn was mixing with the influences of new media that to some extent were incorporated into the conservative aims of this genteel literacy, but also, as we shall see, foreshadowed a radical transformation in society and in Sam May's literacy development. Initially, for the young Sam May and his associates, the arrival of radio and film inspired and enhanced writing for purposes of local, oral performances that resembled the old-fashioned circus ("there weren't any live people up there"). At the same time, though, technological innovations brought into the village from the outside new, more abstract genres, new audience configurations, new channels of communication, and new ways of hearing oneself ("You were always comparing yourself to Orson Welles"). As a teenager Sam May set up a "little workshop" in an abandoned garage where he began to build crystal radio sets and where he often recorded thoughts and ideas for inventions in a notebook that he carried with him constantly. But by this time, radio was about to take on yet another kind of meaning for Sam May—and the country. In 1941, only seventeen days after the attack on Pearl Harbor, a correspondence school called the Army Institute was established nearby in Madison, Wisconsin, as part of what Harold F. Clark and Harold S. Sloan describe as an "explosive" growth in technology and military education brought on during and just after the war (1964, p. 22). In a span of a few years, the development of radar, the jet airplane, the first digital computer, and the transistor radio (not to mention the atomic bomb) created nearly instant need for new knowledge and skill, much of it literacy based. (See Ginzberg and Bray [1953, p. 39ff.] for an account of how male illiteracy was constructed as a social problem at the outbreak of World War II.) Graduating from high school in 1942 and planning to enlist, Sam May took courses through the Army Institute, becoming a certified radio repairman by the time he was eighteen. Soon after, he joined the armed services and was assigned to the Army Signal Corps, but, because of a surplus of radio repairmen, he eventually became a fourth-echelon radar technician stationed in Europe. Like other military veterans I have interviewed, Mr. May described his service years as a period of intensified writing, a period especially when learners of new technologies quickly turned around and became the teachers. (See Clark and Sloan [1964] for descriptions of classroom education in the military during and after World War II.) For Mr. May's part, he began writing service manuals and also weekly reports back to the factory where radar equipment was being manufactured. These reports described changes he was making to the equipment. "We were engineering out the mistakes," he explained. While confident of his technical ability, Sam May said he was less satisfied with his ability to write reports, describing his efforts as "perfunctory." "I'd say, 'I changed this resistor to that.' [The form] would ask, 'What was the reason for the change?' and I'd write, 'Because this other one is a mistake.'" Sam May then went on to describe a strategy he developed for acquiring a new kind of technical literacy that his position was demanding. Just as he often had to improvise to keep the radar equipment working, Sam May improvised a method of learning report writing, modeled in fact on his earlier ways of appropriating "manners" in boyhood:

> Other people used to ask my advice a lot, people who were better at phrasing things than I was, and I'd listen to them, especially the officers, I'd listen to them. Or I'd have to discuss what I wanted to do with, say, a lieutenant or a captain. I was just a mere sergeant. These were all college guys and I was, of course, just a high school brat. So I'd listen to how they'd talk with each other and how they would talk to their peers and their minions. So you could sense the correctness of how they phrased things and how they put things. They always knew how to stay on the subject, not get sidetracked. That had something to do with writing.

Sam May eventually became a "college guy," enrolling for four years under the G.I. Bill in the engineering school of his state university. Now an electronics technician, Mr. May said he devotes about 30 percent of the workday to writing, mostly making circuit diagrams (often on blackboards) and writing footnotes or captions for science reports produced in the labs to which he is assigned. At the time of our interview, sixty-seven-year-old Mr. May indicated he did not use a computer available to him at work. "I haven't had time to learn, but I plan to," he said, "because it is very useful. Saves a lot of drafting time." This partial account of one man's literacy learning between the 1920s and 1940s shows in very particular ways how transformations in literacy accompany large-scale economic, technological, and cultural changes and how these transformations are felt within individual lives. We can gauge this change most interestingly in the two episodes in which Sam May recalls emulating the language of the elite: the first, as a farm boy in a context of manners and noblesse oblige in a socially stratified rural village; the second, as a subordinate army officer in an emerging military-industrial context beginning to require even of "mere sergeants" an ability to render technical know-how in professional prose. These scenes speak to the enduring power of dominant classes to define language standards (a power Pierre Bourdieu [1991] has explored in detail); they predict the emerging power of a highly educated, technocratic elite after the war. Most interesting, these accounts also indicate how much the meaning of education and educated language had begun to change by mid-century—shifting from the cultivated talk of the well-bred to the efficient professional prose of the technocrat—thereby altering the paths of upward mobility for people like Sam May. Many of the materials and strategies that Sam May identifies as part of his literacy learning also appear frequently in the stories of others I have interviewed. The accounts suggest that while a society's older forms of literacy may be superseded by new ones, the old ones don't disappear. Print lasts and artifacts accumulate (in fact, that is their appeal and power), littering the material sites of subsequent literacy learning and shaping future interpretations of reading and writing. This holding on or holding over of older literacies is actually an integral part of the way that one generation passes on the fruits of its education to subsequent generations, a process that is at the center of what we think of as the educational advances of the twentieth century and a process that can have both a conservative and a propelling effect. Schooling typically brings into a family's possession books, manuals, typewriters, and the like that then become the first forms of literacy that the next generation encounters. So Sam May recalled how he would "beg a book" from his aunt's collection and how she would reenact her Palmer School handwriting lessons around the dining room table of the family farm. In an interview, Sam May's son, Jonathan, indicated that some of the first books he recalled encountering as a boy were the college textbooks and technical manuals of his parents.

The influence of other people's literacy and artifacts of their literacy move back and forth across generations, sometimes from younger to older. At the time of our interview, for instance, seventy-nine-year-old Emily Staubach had recently acquired the first personal computer of her life, a "hand-me-up" from her professional son, which she was using to write family memoirs. She in turn had passed her old manual typewriter on to her grandchildren to play with. When I asked thirty-four-year-old Jonathan May to recall how he learned to write reports, he replied, "Well, I think I'm learning more now with my own kids going through school." It is through such material channels that the literacy traditions of previous times appear in the present and that formal education accumulates as a resource in middle-class and working-class households. Reading and writing strategies acquired from older (or younger) generations are then reinterpreted and transformed for use in new and different circumstances—as Sam May's search for writing "manners" demonstrated. In fact, the transformation of literacy obtained in one context for use in another was a principal strategy of literacy learning among the people I interviewed and a hallmark of advancing literacy. Sometimes I think what I am seeing and trying to describe are merely diffusions of education and upward mobility in action, the means by which those resources and aspirations translate into specific experiences with literacy. I also think what I am seeing and trying to describe are the things that bring such complexity to contemporary literacy acquisition. Whereas at one time literacy might have been best achieved by attending to traditional knowledge and tight locuses of meaning, literacy in an advanced literate period requires an ability to work the borders between tradition and change, an ability to adapt and improvise and amalgamate.

"How It Manifests Itself on Paper": Literacy Learning in a Civil Rights Era

To see how similar strategies play out in a different set of circumstances, let's take up the example of Jordan Grant, an African American man who was born in 1948 in urban Mississippi and spent most of his growing-up years in a mid-sized city in Tennessee, where his father was the pastor of a renowned C.M.E. church. Both of his parents, who had themselves been children of small-scale farmers, attended college for a few years, and his father had also done some seminary work. In the Grant home was a collection of the father's theological texts, concordances, and various versions of the Bible, as well as a dog-eared volume of *Poems for Life* that Jordan Grant's mother had bought in the 1940s from a door-to-door salesman. Many of Grant's earliest literacy experiences revolved around the institution of the church, beginning at the age of two with the memorization of an Easter pageant speech. He and his four brothers were coached throughout, he recalled, by a mother who was "steeped in the Southern tradition of memorization." He also has vivid memories of watching his father compose sermons in the parsonage by pacing the floor, often with a baby son on his shoulder, rehearsing under his breath. "You could hear the tremor of his voice," Grant remembered. "His eyes would be fixed and he would just be walking around in circles with this sleeping child on his shoulder preaching these sermons. And then at some point he would go to his old Underwood typewriter and start hunting and pecking about." Jordan Grant named this composing technique "clouding up and raining," adding, "I use the same technique that he used when I do presentations." He had equally vivid memories of helping his mother, the church secretary, crank out church bulletins that she composed each week, including the full worship service and responsive readings, on a mimeograph machine that was kept on the porch of the parsonage. Grant described in detail a process of cutting out and pasting stencils and, later, with an electric mimeograph, hanging up sheets of fresh print to dry. He earned a reputation early in life for his essay writing. As an eighth grader he entered a writing contest entitled "On My Career" held among all the black schools citywide. He wrote an essay on why he wanted to be a minister like his father:

> And I won it. I think the top prize was five or ten silver dollars, which in those days was big stuff. There was an article in the paper, and they had my picture and the other winners from the other grade levels. And my father kept that essay in the Bible waiting for me to become a person of the cloth until the day he died.

Later, as a college student in the late 1960s, Jordan Grant took top prize in a national writing contest on "My People and Power" sponsored jointly by *Reader's Digest* and the United Negro College Fund. In accounting for his success as an essay writer, Grant mentioned vague recollections of grade-school lessons on essay structure and topic sentences. But he was "confident" that his father's sermons served as a model for his own writing. In the following excerpt we see how a style of sermon writing that Pastor Grant would have developed during his seminary training impressed its form in dramatic ways on his young son:

> [My father] did neat sermons. And neat means he would always begin with a text and he would actually have a theme for it. So he would say, "Our sermon for the day is entitled," and he would have an actual title for it. And, in the church—this was very profound—the ushers who served in the church would be lined along the walls, two down front, two in the middle, and two in the back. . . . And I remember on [my father] giving the text, the ushers would all turn and all move to the back of the church to be seated. So very profound, dramatic moments. [My father] did not like people who just got up and started preaching without having thought about both the Scripture, typically both an Old and New Testament

scripture, a theme for it, and there would be a beginning, a middle, and an end. What he would do would be to start off with the written word, he'd have the sermon written out. In most of his sermons you see dot, dot, dot, which meant that by that time the Spirit had taken over. He didn't need the text anymore, he'd just go off. And that's when he became the black preacher.

This scene of literacy transmission—from father to son—is layered with a legacy of literacy, race, and religion. By the mid-nineteenth century in America, the ideological connections among religion, literacy, duty, and personhood helped to expose the morally untenable foundations of slavery to members of the white population. At the same time it sowed the seeds of a liberatory literacy spread through a growing network of African American churches, mostly Baptist and Methodist, as well as church-sponsored schools and seminaries (Frazier and Lincoln, 1974; Cornelius, 1992; Daniel, 1925). For generations the ministry was one of the few careers comfortably open to educated African American men. As a descendent of that tradition, Pastor Grant integrated his formal education, with its lingering classical roots, into the worship service of his congregation, impressing exegesis, thematic development, and—in the about-face of the church ushers—a vivid topical structure on a young son watching and listening in a church pew. (See W. A. Daniel's *The Education of Negro Ministers* [1925] for a description of seminary curriculums at the time that Jordan Grant's father would have been attending. For contemporary treatments of the composition of sermons by African American ministers, see Mitchell, 1970; Moss, 2002.)

As a young writer, Jordan Grant could begin to translate a sermonic style learned from his father into secular channels of expression being opened up for African American students by such newly emerging organizations as the United Negro College Fund, which had been established in 1944 as part of a rapid expansion of literacy and educational achievement among African Americans during the first five decades of the twentieth century. (For a profile of African American literacy and educational achievement during this period, see Smythe, 1976, p. 172.) Grant also identified an "enriched vein" of literate experience in the language arts lessons in his segregated schools. Many of his public school teachers had advanced degrees from northern universities, underwritten by southern states that preferred to pay out-of-state tuition for black students rather than desegregate their university systems. He remembered especially poetry lessons and his love for imagery, alliteration, and metaphor. He also learned the debate process during the Kennedy-Nixon presidential campaign, researching and defending Kennedy's position before a schoolwide mock vote. And, he recalled, he wrote an occasional speech as a student government leader. Grant described his adolescence as a period of intense writing that coincided with civil rights activities in his city. By the mid-1960s his father was hosting training sessions at the church, organized by the Student Non-Violent Coordinating Committee and the Southern Christian Leadership Council, in preparation for picketing at downtown stores. Jordan Grant recalled how he and his brother composed messages for picket signs, jazzed up with tempera paint and glitter. "My brother and I did nice work," he smiled. Grant also wrote constantly in private during this period. "Thoughts, ideas, essays," he described. "Obviously in those times I was concerned with the apartheid racism we were experiencing. Everybody was angry about it, frustrated about it. . . . It was an emotionally charged time and you had lots of things to say." Writing became "a vent." "It did not hurt later on to have had those experiences, but at the time you're not thinking of practicing. . . . You used whatever means you could to work off these frustrations," he explained. With his father still waiting for him to become a minister, Grant enrolled in one of the colleges founded by his Methodist denomination and soon found a truer calling in a class in transformational grammar. "The system of language," he extolled. "To find out that it was much more scientific than I had thought . . . It was just a wonderful, wonderful thing." He graduated with a degree in English and, migrating north, became an English teacher in a public school. Then, in the early 1970s, he became the first affirmative action officer in a predominantly white metropolitan school district while pursuing a Ph.D. in school administration at a Midwest research university. It was then that the "flowery English major with the Ciceronian writing style" was put to work writing an affirmative action plan and training manual in a field that never existed before. "There were no prototypes," Grant explained. A district consultant provided some advice; the rest was trial and error. As he described his new identity as a public sector bureaucrat, it was clear that there was more than a little of the black preacher in Jordan Grant: "My memoranda were very long and pretty or piercing or whatever, but they were not typical," he said. Some tension developed with the "hard-nosed administrators":

> I never wanted to write anything that was so dull and deadly that you couldn't flourish every now and then, but the manual was tough for me. . . . The interplay between what I wanted to write and the way I wanted to write it and what they wanted me to write was pretty hard. I remember a couple of times having the writing reviewed and having been told they didn't particularly like it—which also frustrated me because I didn't particularly like the way they wrote.

Grant encountered similar tensions with his dissertation committee of four white male professors. "I was tending to have all these Ciceronian flourishes and lots of words and lots of analogies and lots of imagery and the professors kept saying, 'You're bleeding on the paper. Stop bleeding on the paper. This is a scientific piece of work.'" Grant learned how to compromise, earning his doctorate and serving for several more years as an educational administrator. He then left the public school system to found his own consulting firm. He now writes on virtually a daily basis, preparing presentations in connection

with his work as well as speeches, letters, and occasional grant proposals in connection with his membership in a local civil rights organization. At the time of our interview he was in the midst of writing a
book manuscript on current civil rights issues. He explained that he
works on the book during odd moments in his frequent business
trips, "clouding up and raining" in airplanes and hotel rooms on a
laptop computer that he taught himself to use. He said his fascination
with writing throughout his life has resided ". . . in the power of it. A lot
of times I was surprised and still am surprised about what I just wrote,
how it manifests itself on paper."

Grant grew up in a period of rapid social change among African
Americans, during which time the educational and liberatory tradition of black religion began to find greater secular expression through
the civil rights movement. This transition registers vividly in Grant's
formative literacy experiences. His account helps to underscore that
change is comprised not merely of the pull from the future but also
the push from the past. The orbit of the Protestant church, so instrumental in the dissemination of basic literacy among white and black
Americans in previous times, continued in the mid-twentieth century
to influence Grant's writing development as he saw church-related
work being done in his household and as he absorbed the oral and
oratorical traditions of black preaching. It was a tradition that he was
able to translate into literacy success in his segregated schools (and
uses now in his professional presentations). As in the case of Sam May,
Jordan Grant's earliest literacy memories exhibit residual influences
of the educational experiences of previous generations, including his
parents and other adult teachers. Classical motifs, memorization,
poetry, debate, and sentence diagramming mingled with emergent
studies such as transformational grammar to form his orientation
to writing. Although school segregation left many African American
students in poor schools with poorly educated teachers, Grant experienced another aspect of this constriction: a concentration of talented

and highly educated teachers produced especially in the last, most desperate years of legal segregation. (See Ginzberg and Bray [1953, p. 192ff.] for an account of the relatively large expenditures some southern states approved for segregated black schools in the years just prior to Brown *v.* Board of Education.) As the radical successes of the civil rights movement of the 1950s and 1960s were domesticated in the 1970s by federal legislation and government oversight of education and employment, new bureaucratic genres like "the affirmative action plan" began to emerge. Amid racial and regional tensions, the adult Jordan Grant found himself trying to integrate his southern, black, sermonic writing style into a northern, white, bureaucratic, and scientific style—a quintessential demonstration of the political struggle still at play as an aftermath of official integration. Now an independent human resources consultant primarily in the private sector, Grant continues to work on developing a professional language that leaves room for the part of himself he calls "the artist." Boxes of his informal writings continue to pile up in the basement of his home, along with a collection of his late father's sermons.

Accumulating Literacy: Implications for Theory

In *The Importance of Illiteracy,* a wise little book written at mid-century, M. M. Lewis suggested that sharply rising concerns about illiteracy around that time were actually indications of the success of literacy in spreading and escalating in value. He pointed out how the social significance of literacy is itself a contributing factor in illiteracy, as spiraling expectations for achievement contribute to the shame and frustration of those who fall below the standard (1953, p. 98). Lewis's book is intriguing because it draws attention to the effects created by a surplus of literacy in this century, even when contemplating the phenomenon of illiteracy. That is, Lewis asks that we entertain the paradoxes that an advancing literacy presents, including the possibility that achievements and failures in reading and writing are caused in some ways by the same conditions. While this chapter has focused on successful responses to an advancing literacy, the interviews I have conducted overall confirm that attempts to acquire reading and writing—unsuccessful as well as successful—take shape in response to a burgeoning of literacy and its enterprises. This accumulation of literacy provides an increasingly intricate set of incentives, sources, and barriers for learning to read and write, the negotiation of which becomes a large part of the effort of becoming (and staying) literate. We are familiar enough with some aspects of this accumulation: it is easily apparent that both Sam May and Jordan Grant, for instance, were swept up educationally and economically into the growth of a technocratic, documentary society after World War II—a kind of second phase of mass literacy that has been creating a higher demand for producers (and not just consumers) of writing. This aspect of accumulating literacy plays heavily in the anxious talk about "the literacy crisis." What we have paid less attention to, however, are the specific contexts that allow rapid changes in literacy and literacy standards to take place, particularly the contexts that provide interpretive materials that people use to respond to (and resist) such changes. These contexts are characterized by latent forms of older, residual literacies that are at play alongside emerging ones. Rapid changes in literacy and education may not so much bring rupture from the past as they bring an accumulation of different and proliferating pasts, a piling up of literate artifacts and signifying practices that haunt the sites of literacy learning. These complicated amalgamations of literacy's past, present, and future help to formulate the interpretive opportunities and complexities facing current generations of literacy learners.

These characteristics of accumulating literacy could be better accommodated in school, simply by beginning to recognize the historical conditions of literacy more fully and consciously. Traditionally, schools have seen their mission as disseminating literacy to each new generation, but what does that mean in a culture where sources of print and literacy—not to mention education itself—are so ubiquitous? Lately there has been more understanding of how particular forms of school-based literacy compete with popular forms, yet the interviewing I am conducting suggests a more complicated picture than that. Whether it be the penmanship lessons Sam May received in his farmhouse, the Orson Welles inflections in his poetry recitations, the office equipment on Jordan Grant's porch, the black southern sermonic style that showed up in school administration memos in the north, or the old engineering manuals that Jonathan May found on the bookshelves in his home, there is much more interpenetration and overlapping of influences as people crisscross among various literacy-based institutions in the course of their normal lives. From this perspective we might begin to see how both "school-based" and "home-based" literacies form and function within larger historical currents.

We can also begin to see how the role of the school in an advanced literate age can be reconceptualized to help students at all levels detect the residual, emergent, and often conflicted contexts of literacy that form their world. Especially important is the ideological potency of literacy materials that come into people's lives and into the scenes of their learning. Materials to some degree always will reflect how individuals, including students, are intersecting at a certain time with the ongoing, official history of mass literacy and the institutions that have controlled it. Because written materials tend to accumulate as household possessions, as forms of inheritance, and because they accumulate as well in the form of remembered readings or writings, these intersections with the history of literacy can be quite complex processes of projection and retrospection. And, while written materials always carry traces of the grand history of official literacy, they also can be infused, as we have seen, with family histories and autobiographical constructions. Important too is the realization that the history of literacy at any moment is always carrying along a complex, sometimes cacophonous mix of fading and ascending materials, practices, and ideologies. Literacy is always in flux. Learning to read and write necessitates an engagement with this flux, with the layers of literacy's past, present, and future, often embodied in materials and tools and just as often embodied in the social relationships we have with the people who are teaching us to read and write. Indeed, as changes in literacy have speeded up in the twentieth century, literate ability has become more and more defined as the ability to position and reposition oneself amidst literacy's recessive and emergent forms. This chapter has only begun to scratch the surface of accumulating or advancing literacy. Yet to be treated, among other things, are the profound effects of electronic media, including television and computers, as well as the meanings of language diversity and immigration in an advanced literate society. But at this point in the investigation I lean, with M. M. Lewis, toward the proposition that problems with reading and writing are less about the lack of literacy in society than about the surplus of it. Being literate in the late twentieth century has to do with being able to negotiate that burgeoning surplus.

References

Bourdieu, Pierre. *Language and Symbolic Power*. Cambridge, Mass.: Harvard University Press, 1991.

Clark, Harold F., and Sloan, Harold S. *Classrooms in the Military: An Account of Education in Armed Forces of the United States*. New York: Teachers College Press, 1964.

Cochran-Smith, Marilyn. *The Making of a Reader*. Norwood, N.J.: Ablex, 1984.

Cornelius, Janet Duitsman. *"When I Can Read My Title Clear": Literacy, Slavery and Religion in the Antebellum South*. Columbia: University of South Carolina Press, 1992.

Cremin, Lawrence A. *American Education: The Metropolitan Experience*. New York: Harper & Row, 1988.

Daniel, William A. *The Education of Negro Ministers*. New York: George H. Doran, 1925.

Frazier, Franklin E., and Lincoln, Eric C. *The Negro Church in America/The Black Church Since Frazier*. New York: Schocken, 1974.

Ginzberg, Eli, and Bray, Douglas W. *The Uneducated*. New York: Columbia University Press, 1953.

Heath, Shirley Brice. *Ways with Words*. New York: Cambridge University Press, 1984.

Landes, William, and Solomon, Lewis. "Compulsory Schooling Legislation." *Journal of Economic History*, 1972, *32*, 54–91.

Lewis, Morris Michael. *The Importance of Illiteracy*. London: George G. Harrap, 1953.

Mitchell, Henry H. *Black Preaching*. Philadelphia: J. B. Lippincott, 1970.

Moss, Beverly. *A Community Text Arises*. Creskill, N.J.: Hampton Press, 2002.

Resnick, Daniel. "Historical Perspectives on Literacy and Schooling." In Stephen R. Graubard (ed.), *Literacy: An Overview by 14 Experts*. New York: Noonday Press, 1991.

Resnick, Lauren. *Education and Learning to Think*. Washington, D.C.: National Academy Press, 1987.

Smythe, Mabel M. (ed.). *The Black American Reference Book*. Englewood Cliffs, N.J.: Prentice Hall, 1976.

4

Remembering Writing, Remembering Reading

A WOMAN BORN IN A WISCONSIN MILL TOWN IN 1968 said her earliest memory of writing was making marks and scratches on the door of a bedroom she shared with four sisters. She did it, she said, "Because I wanted my mom's attention. She was constantly reading, and I think I wanted her to see my writing." Another young Wisconsin woman, raised on a small and sometimes struggling dairy farm, recalled picking up the evening newspaper to read and finding her father's nervous budget calculations penciled all over the margins. A third woman of similar age, raised in the suburbs of Chicago, remembered secretly taking from her mother's purse an envelope on which her mother's signature was written. Alone, she began to copy the signature, "trying desperately not to get caught." She was, in fact, discovered by family members. But, she said, "Instead of being punished for practicing my art of forgery, my beautiful and skillful penmanship was celebrated." These three brief anecdotes stand out for me because they say complicated things about writing-reading relationships that typically have not been treated in the literature on the subject. While various researchers and pedagogues have argued that reading and writing are deeply related language processes, their conceptions typically stress the cognitive similarities and interdependency of the two processes, how both involve the marshalling of particular kinds of prior knowledge or prior experiences with texts, and how both involve fusing personal visions and intentions with the constraints of public contexts and conventions. Researchers have considered, for instance, the readerly dimensions of writing or vice versa (Tierney and Pearson, 1984; Langer, 1986; Bartholomae and Petrosky, 1986; Haas and Flower, 1988; Spivey, 1990). Others have explored how reading can enhance writing and vice versa (Petrosky, 1982; Petersen, 1982; Salvatori, 1983; Elbow, 1993). Or how writers and readers envision each other's motives and moves (Flower, 1988; Vipond and Hunt, 1984; Nystrand, 1990; Brandt, 1990; Hatch, Hill, and Hayes, 1993). Or how people read to write (Smith, 1983; Bereiter and Scardamalia, 1984; Greene, 1992; Flower and others, 1990). Or how they write to read (Chomsky, 1979; Ferreiro and Teberosky, 1982; Harste, Woodward, and Burke, 1984; for a full treatment of these issues, see Ackerman, 1991).

Such studies have been useful for enriching conceptions of literacy and literacy development and for encouraging more conscious pedagogy in English classrooms. Yet the conceptions of reading and writing that underlie these studies do not often begin with the ways that reading and writing actually enter people's lives. These investigations have mostly focused on reading and writing as processes of meaning making, emphasizing the role of textual language in those processes. The interest is in how people make meaning *through* reading and writing. Only incidentally might these studies consider how people make meaning *of* reading and writing. In fact, even ethnographic studies about the functions and uses of literacy in households (for instance, Heath, 1983; Fishman, 1988; Taylor and Dorsey Gaines, 1988) could not wholly do justice to the complexities involved when a preschooler takes up writing to displace her mother's reading, or when a daughter decodes her father's burdens along with the nightly news, or when a child's first attempt at *imitatio* begins with the guilt of theft.

Studies of children's literacy development typically assume the salutary effects of seeing parents reading or writing at home. But the stories above ask that we consider how parental literacy, at least at times, can be a sign or source of trouble for children. They ask us to consider how writing might develop in rivalry to reading. Above all they draw our attention to the fact that what motivates and brings meaning to acts of reading or writing may not always be texts. Instead, much of learning to read and write involves learning the possible attitudes that can be taken toward these two activities, which are often more separate and competing than we may sometimes want to admit.

In this chapter I explore relationships between writing and reading as they emerge in autobiographical accounts of literacy development. My discussion will focus on the differences in cultural attitudes and affective circumstances surrounding people's memories of their literacy experiences. In 1992–93 I audiotaped interviews with forty residents of Dane County, Wisconsin, people who represented a broad cross-section of the population in terms of age, race and ethnicity, place of birth, educational level, and occupation. Volunteers came from nursing homes, housing projects, social service agencies, schools, senior citizen centers, unions, and religious groups, as well as through informal networks of associates. They included adults with Ph.D.s and adults who did not finish grade school. They ranged in age from ninety-six to ten and represented, among others, teachers, farmers, bus drivers, salespeople, maintenance workers, technicians, poets, journalists, government workers, homemakers, secretaries, lawyers, artists, postal workers, executives, home health aides, students, the retired, the disabled, and the un- and underemployed. I spoke with people from one to three hours, usually in their homes. In this chapter, their pseudonyms will be used.

The main purpose of the interviews was to explore literacy learning as it has occurred across the twentieth century. Toward that aim, the interviews focused on what people could remember about learning to read and write across their lifetimes, particularly the occasions, people, materials, and motivations involved in the processes. I also asked about the uses and purposes of literacy at various stages of people's lives. As I began to sort out the interview material, I was struck by pronounced differences between the ways people remembered early reading and early writing. They discussed them differently and seemed to value them differently. Differences especially pertained to the settings in which early reading and writing were remembered to have occurred, as well as the personal and cultural significance assigned to each. Further, while many people thought reading inspired and informed their writing development, it was not the case for everybody. In fact, in few cases did discoveries about the connection between reading and writing proceed smoothly. In the following discussion I will attempt to explain the patterns of differences that emerged in the interviews, speculate about the causes and effects of these differences, and then say something about the implications for research and teaching in writing.

Cultural Dissociations of Reading and Writing

What most surprised me in the interviews was how differently people described the settings of early reading and writing and the feelings surrounding their early encounters with each. On the one hand, although there were some exceptions, people typically remembered their first reading experiences as pleasurable occasions, endorsed if not organized by adults. On the other hand, many early writing experiences, particularly those set outside of school, were remembered as occurring out of the eye of adult supervision, and they often involved feelings of loneliness, secrecy, and resistance. Further, whereas reading with children and encouraging them to read was regarded as part of normal parental responsibilities in many working-class and middle-class families, teaching or encouraging writing (beyond showing very young children how to form letters or checking the spelling on homework assignments) was nearly unheard of and sometimes actively avoided by many of these same families.

The Prestige of Reading

Three-quarters of the people I spoke with said that reading and books were actively endorsed in their households. Mostly this endorsement took the form of being read to by parents (usually mothers), grandparents, or older siblings, usually at bedtime or naptime and often in the presence of other family members. The vividness of early reading memories suggests their importance and their association with pleasure and family intimacy. For instance, Betty MacDuff, a sixty-eight-year-old retired journalist, whose father's education had ended in third grade, recalled her mother reading to both her and her father, whether it was from *Hans Brinker* and *Five Little Peppers and How They Grew* or the "A" volume of the 1936 *Compton's Encyclopedia*. Blanche Hill, a fifty-year-old American Indian who led an otherwise stressful childhood, has pleasurable memories of her widowed mother reading to her and her older brother. She recalled:

> She used to have a big, old storybook. I kind of wish I had it today, but I don't. My brother and I would jump into bed and that would be our entertainment. She'd read stories from the book. And it was just like they were alive. I can still see some of the pictures even now.

In several households, reading religious materials was part of a family routine or holiday ritual. There was only one book in the house of former Missouri sharecropper Johnny Ames, who was born in 1950. The book was the Bible, from which his grandmother would read parables to her children and grandchildren. Another Missouri man of similar age, this one from a St. Louis suburb, remembered having to remain at the supper table after the meal was over to listen to his father read from a book of Bible stories. A twenty-year-old rural Wisconsin man recalled that his mother cut out Christmas stories that appeared in serial form in the local newspaper, pasted them into book form, and read the stories to the family each Christmas Eve thereafter.

In other homes secular reading predominated, and reading story-books or comic books was regarded as a form of entertainment or relaxation. Reading to preschool children cut across class, race, and generation, and included families in which parents had fewer than eight years of schooling or had emigrated from non-English-speaking countries. (Absence of reading to children, however, did seem concentrated in poor households where parents were not native speakers of English, had scant education, or were self-employed in primarily outdoor occupations, such as farming.) In a few cases, parents did not read to children but did give them books. A twenty-three-year-old Hmong man, now a college student, recalled his father instructing him to read an English picture dictionary that had been purchased by their American sponsors. A thirty-three-year-old Chicago-born woman, the daughter of a single mother who worked as a cook, remembered her mother dropping her off, along with her siblings, in front of the downtown library and urging them to go inside.

All parents were perhaps not as conscientious as the mother of eighteen-year-old Rebecca Howard who, when she went to the hospital to give birth to Rebecca, packed children's books to read to her. Nevertheless, reading and the teaching of reading were widely considered as a normal part of the responsible care of young children in many households. The heavy hand of mothers in organizing book-based activities especially indicates the close association between reading and child rearing. Buying books, particularly children's books, was another indication of the value that surrounds exposing children to reading. Among the forty people I interviewed, buying books and magazines was actually more common than going to a library. Where people could not afford bookstore prices, they purchased used books at garage sales, secondhand shops, or library discard sales. Books were frequently kept in prominent locations around a home. Recounting the contents of a room in his house called "the library," Jan Holstrom, who was born in 1958 in Madison, Wisconsin, said:

> My parents had a lot of their college manuals left over, technical manuals. Mom had her x-ray books and a few of the classics. There was *Huckleberry Finn*. You could find him pretty easy. And they are all still there. I don't think they ever threw a book out or gave one away.

In other families, preservation took the form of passing books to younger children in other branches of the family or saving the children's books of one generation to be given eventually to grandchildren.

Books also were given as gifts. Several rural people recounted especially how urban relatives, usually of a higher economic station, would send them fine books on birthdays or at Christmas. Mavis Perkins, born in the South in 1942, remembered that one Christmas as a young girl she was given two identical copies of a desk dictionary, one from her father and one from her adult brother. Olga Nelson, born in rural Wisconsin in 1896, told me how, each Christmas, she and her sisters would find an orange and a book in their stockings. For Olga Nelson, books and reading were clearly part of the good stuff, part of the way their finishing-school mother taught Olga and her sisters to distinguish themselves as a little more refined. "We were," she explained, "a reading family." In general, reading was remembered as an activity, indeed a ritual, that was knitted into holiday celebrations as well as into the ordinary routines of daily life. There was a reverence expressed for books and their value and sometimes a connection between reading and refinement or good breeding. Reading was most typically remembered and described as a deeply sanctioned activity in the culture. Jack Wilitz, whose Texas family broke up in 1940 when he was ten years old, went on the road as an itinerant farm worker for the next thirteen years. He always carried a book or two with him to read at night in itinerant labor camps or during breaks. "If you were reading," he said, "people generally left you alone."

The Ambiguity of Writing

While it must be said that the ability to write was regarded as extremely precious to virtually everybody I interviewed, their accounts suggest that writing develops in situations and out of psychological motivations that are saliently, sometimes jarringly, different from those surrounding reading. These differences surfaced in the memories that people had of their own early writing, their memories of how writing was used and modeled by adults in their households, as well as the uses they have made of writing at various times in their lives. Compared to reading, writing seems to have a less coherent status in collective family life, and much early writing is remembered as occurring in lonely, secret, or rebellious circumstances. The difference I am trying to convey is perhaps most drastically captured in this early memory of a forty-three-year-old South Dakota man, Harry Carlton. "I wrote all the bad words that I knew," he said, "on a blackboard that was on an easel while my mother was having card club. I was at one end of the room and all the women were there in the room for cards." Asked to explain his motivation, he continued, "I think it was just a wild juxtaposition that I could be writing all these nasty thoughts with all these people in the room and they didn't know."

While there was a certain thrill retained in Mr. Carlton's memory, more typically, the feelings surrounding early self-sponsored writing are described as lonely. In stark contrast to cozy bedtime reading, a fifty-year-old disabled woman remembered her first writing occurring in a hospital bed when she was four years old and feeling abandoned. Eleven-year-old Michael Murdoch told me he wrote his first story at five when his family moved to a new neighborhood. The story was about a pig who was having trouble making friends. Carla Krauss, a sixty-year-old Midwestern woman, remembered her first poem was inspired by sitting alone on the front steps of her house waiting for her older sister to arrive home from school. It is, of course, likely that these young authors of stories and poems used technical knowledge derived from their reading to create their compositions, but it is note-worthy that the motivations for the writing in these cases were not books and the motivators were not adults. Rather, the occasions and impulses to write emerged from the children's immediate circum-stances and feelings. Whereas people tended to remember reading for the sensual and emotional pleasure that it gave, they tended to remem-ber writing for the pain or isolation it was meant to assuage. People's descriptions of the settings of childhood and adolescent writing—a hospital bed, the front steps of a house, and, in other cases, a garage, a treehouse, and a highway overpass—were degraded versions of domes-ticity, in marked contrast to the memories of pillowed, well-lit fam-ily reading circles described in so many of the interviews. In another twist on writing-reading relationships, several earliest writing memo-ries involved defacement, including defacement of books. "I remember writing in little kids' books," recalled a twenty-two-year-old Wisconsin woman. "We had those hard covered books . . . and I just remem-ber writing 'Brendas' all over the covers." Jan Holstrom, the man I referred to earlier who remembered the contents of his family's library, also remembered getting caught by his displeased mother while he was writing on the library wall. An eighteen-year-old farmer, Susan Parsons, remembered that at the age of three she wrote the word *apple* (learned, she believed, by watching Sesame Street) on the wall of her grandparents' house on the afternoon of her brother's birth. If early urges to write were frequently associated with ambiguous and com-plex motives and feelings, including self-assertion, violation, jealousy, and guilt, adult relationships to youngsters' early writing efforts could also be ambiguous and unpredictable. As we have already seen with the opening signature copying episode, a young forger was surprised when her handwriting was praised. After Susan Parsons's grandparents reprimanded her for writing on the wall, they took a picture of it, an artifact that became part of the legend of Susan's precociousness. And, as a postscript to the card party story, Harry Carlton's mother later would point out to him that the word *butt* is spelled with two t's. These accounts further demonstrate the mixed messages that can encase literacy memories. In these examples, lessons about the proprieties of language correctness or adult delight in literary precociousness are remembered in connection with misbehavior or rebellion.

The ambiguity that surrounded memories of writing actually began at a more fundamental level: with the definition of writing itself. Reading was usually recalled as a clearly demarcated activity; the names of first books, even, in some cases, the first lines of first primers, surfaced in people's descriptions. Memories of writing were decidedly more vague. "It's difficult to remember writing as a separate activity," remarked a sixty-eight-year-old Wisconsin man about his growing-up years. "I don't have memories of people actually sitting down and writing," said a thirty-one-year-old man about his household. More often than not, writing went under the rubrics of "work" or "doing the bills," "doodling," or "homework." Vague definitions of writing posed an interesting problem in the conduct of the interviews. In asking people to describe in general how they learned to write, I deliberately left the term "writing" undefined at the start of each interview. Many people assumed the topic was handwriting, while others equated writing exclusively with literary or creative composition. Many of the latter group initially reported that they did no writing when, in fact, with more probing, I found they used writing for an array of ordinary purposes. This mundane writing was practically invisible to them because in their estimation it did not qualify as writing. A dual association of writing with the invisibly mundane and the creatively elite probably helps to account for the lack of parental endorsement or specific teaching of writing to offspring. Johnny Ames, mentioned earlier in connection with Bible reading by his sharecropper grandmother, said he had no recollection of writing anything as a boy, even though his grandmother, who he said taught him everything he knew, wrote in connection with her work. Probing, I asked:

Would you have seen your grandmother writing?

Yeah, I saw her write.

What would she have been doing?

Well, see, my grandmother's job was to hire people to pick cotton, fill out, do all the figures. She had to put the name of the people, how much they worked, how much they picked a day. Every time they picked she had to weigh the cotton and tally it up at the end of the day, take it to the gin, get it weighed, get the money, pay the people off, and take the rest and turn it in. She had to keep the books for the person she worked for.

Okay, but you don't remember . . .

It was nothing encouraged. There was no encouragement of writing . . . in my household when I was coming up. It was just a necessity for her to do that. . . . I saw her do it, I understood why she was doing it, but there was no encouragement for me to do that.

For Mr. Ames's grandmother, writing was just a necessity for her job and not thought of as a separate activity or skill to be passed along for its own sake, at least not to a young child. Judging from the interviews as a whole, Ames's experience was not all that unique. While adults in many households, as we have seen, considered reading with children to be part of their parental responsibility, they didn't seem to extend that responsibility quite so articulately to writing. Hope Moore, a college graduate who married a college professor and wrote extensively herself while involved in the League of Women Voters, remembered her only child, a daughter, as being "kind of a writer":

Oh, she was really a writer all the way through. She had a long saga about some imaginary girl she wrote. And she did sort of a novel. She called it a novel.

But you didn't teach that explicitly to her?

No. Well, I encouraged her because it kept her busy and it was something to do sometimes. And I thought it was nice that she had that interest. But I never would have said, "Go, write something on your novel." I would never have thought of it.

Carla Krauss, a woman who wrote creatively as a child and went on to attend college, read regularly to her two sons. But she rejected the idea that writing could or should be actively encouraged by parents. Another mother of three, herself a journalist, echoed the reluctance to intervene in what she believed to be a natural and mysterious process. "The ones that had the creative spark did it," she said of her children's writing. Martha Wilcox, who at eight-nine was organizing a lifetime of journal entries, said she always kept the writing her children did at school or home. "But," she said, "I didn't push it." It's interesting to note how a cultural ideal that could have been derived from literary reading—the romantic writer as natural genius—plays out in parents' hands-off attitudes toward children's writing development. Even further, negative stereotypes of the creative writer sometimes translated into active or at least passive discouragement of an offspring's literary pursuits. Heddy Lucas, an eighty-four-year-old émigré from Poland, told me that she read to her only son Benjamin every night before he went to sleep. In an interview later with Benjamin Lucas, who was born in New York in 1936, I learned that he not only read voraciously but also, as a young adult, wrote poetry and plays. I asked him what kind of encouragement there was in his household for writing. He explained:

Not only did I not get encouragement at home, but I got a lot of discouragement because this was something that was so totally an anathema to [my family]. First, they didn't understand it, but what they thought they understood about it was something they identified with poverty and wastefulness.

Similarly, Yi Vang, whose father encouraged him to read an English dictionary, recalled becoming enthused about writing after a course including journal keeping and creative writing taken with a particularly supportive high school teacher. He tried to keep the momentum going on his own during the summer. "I thought maybe I wanted to be a writer," he recalled, "so I would write my stories and it went pretty long. But after a while you ran out of ideas and there was nobody there to help you. There was nobody there to acknowledge you were doing a good job." It is not surprising, given the ambivalence and vagueness that surrounds writing as an activity that developing an identity as a writer is rather difficult. Many people took pride in calling themselves an "avid reader" or "quite a reader" or "always reading." Yet there was reticence among the people I spoke with—including a well-established, published poet—to regard themselves as writers, despite the obvious avidity of their pursuit of writing. Some of this reticence had to do with not seeing writing as an end in itself. Sixty-six-year-old Carla Krauss, who, as I have mentioned, wrote poetry and plays as a schoolgirl and now writes philosophical essays that she shares with close friends, said of her childhood writing: "I enjoyed it. I really had no sense of it as writing at all. It was almost for another purpose." Benjamin Lucas, now a writer and critic, remarked, "I think I never had a sense of myself as a writer. I think I had a sense of myself as wanting to do something that my peers and my family just weren't doing." Bernice King, a former telephone operator who has written fiction and poetry intermittently all of her life, was working on a series of short stories when I interviewed her. I asked her when and how she began to develop an identity as a writer. "I don't think I ever thought about it," she said.

In documenting the ambiguity that seems to surround writing and parental involvement in promoting writing, I do not mean to imply that writing was regarded as unimportant among those I interviewed. In fact, many memories suggest that the products of writing, at least, are highly valued. Children's writing—even more than schoolbooks—is a tangible medium that links home and school. Many people recalled bringing home written projects from school for parents to read and, if the report received a high grade, to display on refrigerators or bulletin boards. When Michael Murdoch wrote his story about the friendless pig, he showed it to his mother who in turn showed it to a teacher for whom she was doing babysitting. Many adults I talked with still had in their possession research papers, family genealogies, and other papers they had composed in grade school and high school. Nor were all early memories of writing charged with ambiguous or difficult feelings. A few individuals indeed described scenes of intimacy and adult sponsorship of writing that resembled accounts of early reading. Ted Anderson, an eighteen-year-old Wisconsin farmer, recalled that he would sit next to his mother as she wrote letters to relatives and pretend to write himself in a small notebook that she had given him for just such occasions. Fifty-year-old Chicago native Bernice King, who now writes fiction, remembered her early interest in a cloisonné pen owned by her schoolteacher grandmother. Her grandmother promised her that she could use the pen if she learned to write certain things. "The first time she let me use it was on my fifth birthday," she recalled, "and it was great, and I've grown to love cloisonné." Writing (at least as it translated into school success or economic gain) also appeared to be encouraged through the giving of gifts. Typewriters were widely purchased by parents and given to offspring (most commonly, the firstborn) before they went off to college or when they enrolled in secretarial courses. Two women I interviewed remembered as teens being given diaries for their birthdays, one by her mother and another by her aunt. Another recent high school graduate was given a journal as a graduation present from her German teacher (in anticipation of the student's planned trip to Germany). But, all in all, diaries and journals were more frequently self-purchased than received as gifts, and writing-related gifts seemed much less prevalent and much less strongly associated with holidays than book giving.

On the whole the status of writing in everyday literacy practices is decidedly more ambiguous and conflicted in comparison to reading. Except for the dutiful thank-you notes or letters home from camp that some people recalled being required to write as children, writing does not appear to play a standard role in the activities or rituals of families, especially in the communal way that reading is. Nor is writing so readily identified as a separate activity. Rather, writing seems to be experienced more as an embedded means than a demarcated end in itself. Writing does not seem to be as broadly sponsored and endorsed by parents; nor does the identity "writer" seem as easily available as the identity "reader."

Reading and Writing Across Generations

Looking more closely at the functions of writing and reading in households reveals how much more stratified writing is than reading, by which I mean more natural opportunities seem to exist to share reading and knowledge about reading across generations than is the case for writing. On the one hand, people I spoke with tended to associate their parents' reading primarily with learning, relaxing, and worshiping—all activities that are equally available to children and adults and that often take place in communal settings. On the other hand, parents' writing was mostly associated with earning money, paying bills, and maintaining communication with distant family relations—activities more strictly in the purview of adults. As we have already seen, people were aware, as children, of the functions of their parents' work-related writing, but that kind of writing usually remained out of the realm of most children. Eighty-three-year-old Hope Moore did recall helping her grocer father sort and record checks at their kitchen table, and twenty-year-old William Bussler had close-up memories of his father's dairy delivery records because he used to ride along on the route. But in most cases children were not really invited to participate in their parents' writing nor were they ready or natural audiences for it. The woman who inadvertently had become an audience of her father's writing left on the daily newspaper said she mostly ignored her parents when they were doing figures or writing letters to relatives. It was not unusual for children of professional fathers to say that their fathers' work-related writing went on behind closed doors in rooms off-limits to children.

While it was rare for children to read their parents' writing, it was quite common for children to read their parents' magazines. *Saturday Evening Post, Look, Reader's Digest, Ebony, Jet, Ladies' Home Journal,* as well as farming and hunting magazines, were standard reading fare for many children and adolescents. But there was nothing really comparable on the writing side. Parents may have read to children, but parents seldom wrote to children (exceptions were two noncustodial parents who lived apart from their children). One woman did tell me that when the oldest of her seven siblings was drafted into the Army during the Vietnam War, her mother organized a letter-writing effort by which mother and children took turns writing a weekly letter. Overall, though, writing appeared to be more segregated and stratified between adults and children than was reading.

The link between writing and adult work was not the only cause for this segregation. Rather, the secrecy and privacy that surrounded many forms of writing diminished occasions for teaching and learning. Two people I interviewed reported that their parents wrote poetry (one a day-laboring mother and the other a dray-operating father), but, interestingly, neither of these people were aware of their parents' creative writing until they had themselves become adults. Thirty-six-year-old Anthony Brugnoli told me when I interviewed him that his father had just been sent a journal that had been kept by Anthony's grandfather in Italy and that he and his father were arranging to have it translated. An eighty-four-year-old retired garment worker, who rarely has written throughout her life, confided to me that she was writing a long, autobiographical letter to her grandchildren but that she did not wish the existence of the letter to be revealed until after her death. The writing mentioned above all may have been kept secret as a kind of legacy meant for eventual disclosure, but many of the people I interviewed had at some time in their lives written things explicitly meant to be kept from others. Miles Murphy remembered a retreat he made as a teenager in the 1930s out of an old car seat set up in a barn where he wrote thoughts and plans in a notebook. Diaries were almost always explicitly associated with secrecy. Carla Krauss said that at age nine or ten she became "intrigued by the idea of having secret diaries." Blanche Hill, the woman with warm memories of storybook reading with her mother and brother, recalled: "There was an old, dilapidated garage in the back of one house we lived in and the ceiling was coming down. I used to keep my diary up there. I'd write in there and keep it up there so nobody would see it." Alison Wilhem, the girl who copied her mother's signature in secret, went on, as a grade schooler, to write stories in secret. "I rarely told anyone and kept my folders under the mattress."

Several people mentioned that diary keeping or private writing ended bitterly when a sibling or someone else discovered and violated the secrecy of their writings. Many people I interviewed reported using private writing to purge feelings, primarily anger or grief. Much of this writing was never shown to anyone and was in fact destroyed (certainly another obstacle for the passing along of knowledge about writing). Using writing as a "purge" or "vent" (frequently used expressions) was especially common among white and black women and among black men who I interviewed. This writing tended to occur at times of crisis: death, divorce, romantic loss, incarceration, war, and other forms of social upheaval. Sixty-seven-year-old Eva O'Malley remembered writing a lot during her divorce and still resorts to writing "to get through a lot of feelings of family situations . . . I just write it out, and when I'm done I throw it away because it's down." "I was having a problem coping with different things happening in my family," said Susan Parsons about her parents' divorce when she was nine. "I would write them down as to how I felt and it seemed to help." Forty-six-year-old Darlinda Scott, sometimes in the company of her friends, would write down her experiences with job discrimination in the form of protest letters that she would not mail. Jordan Grant, born in 1948, was the son of a pastor of a C.M.E. church in Tennessee. The church was the site of much organizing of civil rights protests in the 1950s and 1960s. "It was an emotionally charged time and you had a lot of things to say," he explained. He said he wrote constantly during this period as "a vent," as "an alternative to hitting people." Johnny Ames, who left school after eighth grade functionally illiterate, spent seventeen years in prison, where he taught himself to read and write and earned an associate's degree as a paralegal technician. He said he started writing regularly after he moved from a maximum- to a minimum-security prison. "I saw things that didn't set right with what I felt," he explained. "I'd write my feelings about that and throw them away." In focusing so heavily on connections between writing and secrecy, I do not wish to overlook that much reading does go on in secrecy and privacy, and that the history of censorship and punishment around reading is at least as long and as volatile as it is around writing. In a handful of cases, people I interviewed were at least as apt to associate reading with escape and resistance as others did writing (see Radway, 1984).

Sometimes people's choices of reading material got them in trouble at home or in school. Jordan Grant, for instance, remembered a minor inquisition occurring when his father noticed a book with the word *murder* in the title among the books that, as a young teen, he had brought home from the library. A forty-two-year-old woman from the

East Coast recalled that while in high school her paperback copy of *Naked Lunch* was confiscated by a study hall monitor. But what I want to emphasize is a salient and inescapable disparity that arose in the interviews having to do with the way children and adults relate to each other through reading and writing. It appears that what gives writing its particular value for people—its usefulness in maintaining material life, withholding experience for private reflection, and resisting conformity and control—are the very qualities that make writing a problematic practice for adults to pass on to children or for children to share easily with adults. Paradoxically, writing remains more invisible than reading, both because of how it is embedded in mundane, workaday concerns and because of how it is surrounded by privacy, secrecy, and suspicion. Consequently, parents and children have fewer ways of seeing, naming, and talking about writing than appears to be the case for reading (see Langer, 1989). We can say, then, that not only do people spend considerably more time reading in their lives than writing (a fact that has been used to account for differentials in people's reading and writing abilities), but also that opportunities for learning about the acts and activities of writing are usually fainter in comparison to reading.

Writing and Reading Relationships in School

The story of writing-reading relationships changes somewhat when memories turn to literacy practices in school, where prestige around reading and ambivalence around writing play out in a somewhat different and somewhat paradoxical configuration. Historical accounts of writing-reading relationships in school typically stress their structural dissociation (a split that goes back to the earliest beginnings of literacy teaching in churches and schools). Writing almost always plays second fiddle to reading in terms of the time and resources spent on each (Laqueur, 1976; Furet and Ozouf, 1982; Monaghan and Saul,

1987). For the most part, specific memories held by people I interviewed across the generations suggest that reading and writing were
actually often linked in school assignments, but usually in a way that
subordinated writing and in a way by which students could not necessarily appreciate underlying similarities in the two activities.

As most people recalled school assignments, writing seemed to
be introduced in order to induce, support, or verify reading (see also
Slevin, 1986; Berlin, 1990; Miller, 1991; Elbow, 1993). Harry Carlton,
schooled in South Dakota in the 1950s and 1960s, remembered doing
no writing through junior high school save for making elaborate out-
lines of assigned reading. Among those who do recall writing, book
reports were the most ubiquitously remembered assignments. A fifty-
year-old rural man spoke for many when he described how, in third
or fourth grade, students "used to get a certificate if we read so many
books. But we did have to write a report on these books to get our
star." Expository reports, usually on animals or states, were also commonly remembered across the generations. Students began by going
to the school library, reading on their subject, and then producing an
essay that usually resembled the texts they had read, primarily encyclopedia entries. A man born in 1945 and schooled in a university community in Missouri recalled reading Dick and Jane stories in kindergarten
and then receiving a lined sheet of paper with printed prompts inviting him to invent simple stories making himself, his family, and his
pet the protagonists. Jordan Grant, educated in segregated schools in
Arkansas and Tennessee during the 1950s and early 1960s, remembered
a major poetry project in high school. The unit began with extensive
lessons on the technical vocabulary and conventional forms of poetry.
Next was a trip to the woodworking shop or home economics room
where students designed and produced book covers. After that, students filled their books with five or six poems by white poets, five or
six poems by black poets, and, then, in the back of the book, a number

of their own poems in the different forms that had been studied. We might say in these assignments text structures were highlighted and students were invited to occupy positions of authorship. But Shirley Brice Heath (1981) has conjectured that the emphasis in the schools on literary and expository writing, with a stress on individual author-ship and professional models, was actually a way of imposing elitist values and domesticating amateur, popular forms of writing that had flourished in earlier times. Linking writing to reading, then, was a way to curtail or control writing, not necessarily to develop it. Certainly an emphasis on writing to pay homage or writing to validate one's read-ing may be a reason that, as we shall see here, few people attributed their writing development primarily to the reading that was done in such explicitly linked school assignments.

Finally, some attention must be paid to a complicating factor in memories of school-based reading and writing—namely, the many unofficial literacy events and literacy lessons that people vividly and sometimes painfully recalled. In this unofficial curriculum, so to speak, writing once again seemed to separate significantly from read-ing as a sub rosa activity. Several people I spoke with remembered writing satires and spoofs of poetry and other texts assigned in school. One man remembered writing satiric newspaper accounts (includ-ing unflattering items about his teacher) and passing them furtively around his fourth-grade classroom. Several people, like fifty-year-old Charlie Smith, associated note passing in school with "big secrets," some remembering that they resorted to pseudonyms or secret codes in case notes were apprehended by teachers or otherwise fell into the wrong hands. Writing also was discussed as more highly censored (at least, more directly censored) than reading. Rebecca Howard, for instance, recalled her high school principal closing down the stu-dent newspaper on which she had been serving as one of the editors because of a controversial article that the students had insisted on printing. The mixed messages that can surround memories of writing in school were perhaps best captured in the memory of Michelle Friedman, who will never forget that "horrible moment" in sixth grade when she was caught passing a note about one of her classmates, a note that "was not very nice." "Mrs. C _____ seized the note from my hand," she said, "and after class warned me gravely, 'Never write things down, Michelle, never!'"

Conclusion

In tracing the cultural dissociations of reading and writing as they emerged in these interviews, I join others who have lately called for a broadening of the scope by which we study literacy practices and the need to understand school-based writing in terms of larger cultural, historical, and economic currents. Much wisdom already has come from such an expanded view, particularly in appreciating various clashes between schooled and nonschooled literacy, the public and private, the dominant and the marginalized. The interviews that I have collected do not dramatically point to ruptures or differences between the literacies of home and school. (Indeed, as formal education accumulates in middle-class and working-class families in the twentieth century, the effects of that education inevitably flavor the early home literacy experiences of subsequent generations.) Rather, I have appreciated how school and home practices together participate in the broader cultural diffusions of literacy in the twentieth century, a process that multiplies the contexts in which the young encounter and acquire reading and writing. That historical process is what most deserves our attention. Fern Kaplan, born in 1965 near Washington, D.C., recalled how, at seven or eight, she read for the first time the heavily censored FBI file concerning her father, an attorney disbarred unfairly during the McCarthy investigations. The only thing she remembers about the conversation afterwards was her father telling her that she should always put a date on anything she wrote, "a compulsion," she said, "that has stayed with me." If we are going to understand better what literacy instruction represents to students in the future and how it sometimes, inexplicably, can go awry, it is especially important to know about the settings in which the knowledge of reading and writing have come to them and the significance implied in those settings. We must understand better what is compelling literacy as it is lived.

References

Ackerman, John. "Reading, Writing, and Knowing: The Role of Disciplinary Knowledge in Comprehension and Composing." *Research in the Teaching of English,* 1991, *25,* 133–178.

Bartholomae, David, and Petrosky, Anthony. *Facts, Artifacts, and Counterfacts: Theory and Method for a Writing Course.* Upper Montclair, N.J.: Boynton, 1986.

Bereiter, Carl, and Scardamalia, Marlene. "Learning About Writing from Reading." *Written Communication,* 1984, *1,* 163–188.

Berlin, James. "Writing Instruction in School and College English, 1890–1985." In James J. Murphy (ed.), *A Short History of Writing Instruction from Ancient Greece to Twentieth-Century America.* Davis, Calif.: Hermagoras Press, 1990, pp. 183–222.

Brandt, Deborah. *Literacy as Involvement: The Acts of Writers, Readers, and Texts.* Carbondale: Southern Illinois University Press, 1990.

Chomsky, Carol. "Approaching Reading Through Invented Spelling." In Lauren B. Resnick and Patricia A. Weaver (eds.), *Theory and Practice in Early Reading,* Vol. 2. Hillsdale, N.J.: Erlbaum, 1979.

Elbow, Peter. "The War Between Reading and Writing and How to End It." *Rhetoric Review,* 1993, *12,* 524.

Ferreiro, Emilia, and Teberosky, Ana. *Literacy Before Schooling.* (Karen G. Castro, Trans.) Exeter, N.H.: Heinemann, 1982.

Fishman, Andrea. *Amish Literacy: What and How It Means.* Portsmouth, N.H.: Heinemann, 1988.

Flower, Linda. "The Construction of Purpose in Reading and Writing." *College English,* 1988, *50,* 528–550.

Flower, Linda, and others. *Reading to Write: Exploring a Cognitive and Social Process.* New York: Oxford University Press, 1990.

Furet, Francois, and Ozouf, Jacques. *Reading and Writing: Literacy in France from Calvin to Jules Ferry.* New York: Cambridge University Press, 1982.

Greene, Stuart. "Mining Texts in Reading to Write. *Journal of Advanced Composition,* 1992, *12,* 151–170.

Haas, Christina, and Flower, Linda. "Rhetorical Reading Strategies and the Construction of Meaning." *College Composition and Communication,* 1988, *39,* 167–184.

Harste, Jerome C., Woodward, Virginia A., and Burke, Carolyn L. *Language Stories and Literacy Lessons.* Exeter, N.H.: Heinemann, 1984.

Hatch, Jill A., Hill, Charles A., and Hayes, John R. "When the Messenger Is the Message." *Written Communication,* 1993, *10,* 569–598.

Heath, Shirley Brice. "Toward an Ethnohistory of Writing in American Education." In Marcia Farr Whiteman (ed.), *Writing: The Nature, Development, and Teaching of Written Communication.* Vol. *1.* Hillsdale, N.J.: Erlbaum, 1981, pp. 25–45.

Heath, Shirley Brice. *Ways with Words.* New York: Cambridge University Press, 1983.

Langer, Judith A. *Children Reading and Writing: Structures and Strategies.* Norwood, N.J.: Ablex, 1986.

Langer, Judith A. "Reading, Writing, and Understanding." *Written Communication,* 1989, *6,* 66–85.

Laqueur, Thomas. *Religion and Respectability: Sunday Schools and Working Class Culture 1780–1850.* New Haven, Conn.: Yale University Press, 1976.

Monaghan, E. Jennifer, and Saul, E. Wendy. "The Reader, the Scribe, the Thinker: A Critical Look at the History of American Reading and Writing Instruction." In Thomas S. Popkewitz (ed.), *The Formation of School Subjects: The Struggle for Creating an American Institution.* New York: Palmer, 1987, pp. 85–122.

Miller, Susan. *Textual Carnivals: The Politics of Composition.* Carbondale: Southern Illinois University Press, 1991.

Nystrand, Martin. "Sharing Words: The Effects of Readers on Developing Writers." *Written Communication,* 1990, *7,* 324.

Petersen, Bruce T. "Writing About Responses: A Unified Model of Reading, Interpretation, and Composition." *College English,* 1982, *44,* 459–468.

Petrosky, Anthony. "From Story to Essay: Reading and Writing." *College Composition and Communication,* 1982, *33*(February), 19–36.

Radway, Janice. *Reading the Romance: Women, Patriarchy, and Popular Literature.* Chapel Hill: University of North Carolina Press, 1984.

Salvatori, Mariolina. "Reading and Writing a Text: Correlations Between Reading and Writing Patterns." *College English,* 1983, *45,* 657–666.

Slevin, James. "Connecting English Studies." *College English,* 1986, *48,* 543–550.

Smith, Frank. "Reading Like a Writer." *Language Arts,* 1983, *60,* 558–567.

Spivey, Nancy. "Transforming Texts: Constructive Processes in Reading and Writing." *Written Communication,* 1990, *7,* 256–287.

Taylor, Denny. *Family Literacy: Young Children Learning to Read and Write.* Exeter, N.H.: Heinemann, 1983.

Taylor, Denny, and Dorsey Gaines, Catherine. *Growing Up Literate: Learning from Inner City Families.* Portsmouth, N.H.: Heinemann, 1988.

Tierney, Robert J., and Pearson, P. David. "Toward a Composing Model of Reading." In Julie M. Jensen (ed.), *Composing and Comprehending*. Urbana, Ill.: National Council of Teachers of English, 1984.

Vipond, Douglas, and Hunt, Russell. "Point Driven Understanding: Pragmatic and Cognitive Dimensions of Literary Reading," *Poetics*, 1984, *13*(3), 261–277.

5

Writing for a Living

Literacy and the Knowledge Economy

WRITING IS AT THE HEART OF THE KNOWLEDGE ECONOMY. Knowledge-intensive companies account for more than 40 percent of new employment growth during the past fifty years (Stewart, 1997, p. 41). Some analysts estimate that knowledge, most of it codified in writing, now composes about three-fourths of the value added in the production of goods and services (Neef, 1998, p. 4), making it more valuable than land, equipment, or even money. As Stewart (1997) observes,

> Knowledge has become the primary ingredient in what we make, do, buy, and sell. As a result, managing knowledge—finding and growing it, storing it, selling it, sharing it [and, I would add, regulating it]—has become the most important economic task of individuals, businesses, and nations [p. 12].

Although knowledge and literacy are not synonymous, literacy is both a form of knowledge and a way of formalizing knowledge, a means and an end of production. The human skills of literacy make the knowledge economy viable. Writers put knowledge in tangible, and thereby transactional, form (Brandt, 2002). Writing, we might say, is hot property. And as written products become a chief vehicle for economic trade and profit making (and thereby a vehicle for potential impropriety and even crime), work writing itself is becoming subject to greater oversight by government and professional regulators.

My aim in this chapter is to explore this turn of events through the perspectives of people who write for a living. Drawing on in-depth interviews with twelve people, I seek to understand how a growing alignment of writing with productivity and competitiveness relates to contemporary workplace writing practices and the experiences of people situated in writing-intensive positions. Although discussions of the knowledge economy rarely if ever focus explicitly on the role of reading and writing in the making and selling of knowledge, it is vital for researchers in literacy studies to uncover and understand that relationship. Furthermore, interest cannot stop with how literacy is being taken up by the new economy but must extend to how this uptake relates to the possibilities of literacy more broadly. If, as theorists tell us, literacy in a society takes its meanings and consequences from how it is used (Scribner and Cole, 1981; Street, 1995), this relatively new yet robust use of writing to fuel a mass economy could stand to affect the ideological basis of literacy in broad and unforeseen ways.

In the knowledge economy, wealth is created by generating and leveraging knowledge. The term embraces industries that create and sell information or expert knowledge directly as well as those that make products whose chief ingredient is knowledge (for example, genetic testing). The term also embraces the wider role that knowledge plays in increasing innovation and productivity, no matter what the industry (Beniger, 1986; Boisot, 1999; Burton-Jones, 1999). The knowledge economy is associated heavily with brain power, creativity, and other so-called human capital. It is also associated with processes of learning, communication, and social networking, almost always technology-enhanced. The close parallel between descriptions of the knowledge economy and descriptions of literacy (which is itself a form of brain power and human skill closely associated with learning, communication, social networking, and technology) is the intriguing connection pursued here. In the knowledge economy, as Florida (2002) observes, workers "control the means of production because it is inside their heads; they are the means of production" (p. 37). This reliance for productivity on the intimate parts of people's minds, including their ways of communicating, brings a promise of unprecedented investment in the powers of human cognition, learning, and literacy but, at the same time, unprecedented opportunities for intrusion and exploitation.

Writing as the Thing: Manufacturing Texts

My focus here is on what happens to writers and their writing when texts themselves are a chief commercial product of an organization—when such high-stakes factors as corporate reputation, client base, licensing, competitive advantage, growth, and profit rely on what and how people write. In their interviews, writers revealed how larger organizational processes are geared to the production of writing as well as how much investment in time, space, expertise, oversight, and what one writer called "psychological effort" are expended to establish and maintain the integrity of written products. Descriptions of manufacturing-like processes were not uncommon. As Roxanne Richards, a marketing director, said,

> When I write a press release, the actual written document gets rubber-stamped. Then a lawyer reviews it, a technical person reviews it, [the CEO] reviews it and then, believe it or not, the very last person to sign off on it is our regulatory affairs officer.

Even a mundane document such as a press release bobs down a production line, going through the scrutiny of no fewer than four highly paid professionals, each exerting a specialized version of quality control. The highly collaborative nature of workplace writing has been widely observed by researchers (Cross, 1993; Lay and Karis, 1991; Lunsford and Ede, 1990); the connection between collaboration and the high-stakes nature of written products was emphasized repeatedly in the interviews. Securities dealer George Carlisle, branch manager of an investment firm, described the process as follows:

> When you're writing proposals, you're bidding on 10, 30, 40 million-dollar deals. That's serious business. You better pay attention to it. You have to clearly communicate in print before you get the opportunity to communicate by mouth. So the door stays closed unless you are good at communicating in writing. Proposal work is blocked out. We call them power blocks. We just block out a period of time when no one is going to get near us. Seventy percent of proposal writing is done by my associate, and then, we collaborate on what she puts together as well as her team in (central headquarters). And we tend to write and proofread and change and proofread and change until we're sure it's tight.

At Barry Freund's accounting firm, the partners do most of the textual review "because we have more on the line in case something gets us in trouble." Ed Halloran, an educational materials designer, described elaborate, year-long production processes for projects, involving many participants, ranging from consultants to freelancers to editors to attorneys, a process that continued to be tinkered with as the firm grew in experience. As a research assistant in clinical drug trials, registered nurse Pam Collins reported constant oversight of her written work: "There was a representative from the pharmaceutical company called the monitor, and his or her responsibility was to make sure that you followed all the rules," she explained. "They'd come out and look at all the papers." Now, as a development director, Collins says her writing is mostly promotional, yet oversight remains built-in:

> My administrator and I always read each other's writing, and we tease each other because we have red pens. We have the philosophy

that the more eyes that look at something before it goes out, the better. That can sometimes slow our process down, but our administrator says faster is not always better.

Under mandates of the National Association of Securities Dealers, about which more will be said later, investment firm branch manager George Carlisle reads (with the help of a software program) sometimes hundreds of e-mails a day that go in and out of his office. "If a statement isn't consistent with parameters for communication, that would trigger an 'oops, that's not going out,'" he explained. Although writing is generally seen as representation (as records of trades completed, medical interventions completed, and scientific discoveries established), these descriptions suggest how much writing can be the thing, taking its place as a manufactured and inspected object with consequences for an entire concern. As I will explore later, federal agents and other regulators also turn their attention to an organization's written language as a basis not merely for determining compliance but for defining it.

The Toil of Writing: Writers as Mediators and Mediational Means in Production

Understanding writing as a manufacturing process in knowledge work can explain the high levels of collaboration and oversight that occur in workplace writing. It also accounts for the high levels of mediation and synthesis that compose the work of so much contemporary writing. Mediation and synthesis refer to the ways that writers serve as tools of production, transforming complex organizational histories and interests, needs, and constraints into textual form and smelting their awareness of specialized knowledge, regulation, and multiple audiences, constituencies, and competitors into their work processes and products (see Bazerman, 2002, for a fascinating account in this regard of the writing of early knowledge worker Thomas Edison).

Workplace writers can be likened to complex pieces of machinery that turn raw materials (both concrete and abstract) into functional, transactional, and valuable form, often with great expenditures of emotional, psychological, and technical effort. As securities dealer George Carlisle observed in answer to a question about whether he used boilerplate formats in his writing, "You better write with your heart and your brain if you expect to win."

Mediation comprises the hard work of producing writing. In the interviews, it came embedded in writers' accounts of having to translate one form of knowledge into another; to write texts that would be embedded in a larger activity; to ghostwrite or otherwise write (and read) on behalf of abstract or multisourced and sometimes competing interests; to bring the significance of raw facts into a particular context; to reduce text (often reported as being concise); and to walk in other people's shoes either to gain experience needed to write or as a form of audience analysis. Descriptions of what I call mediation and synthesis showed up frequently when writers related what they considered the most difficult and most satisfying aspects of their work as well as when they related occasions of significant conflict and significant learning.

In some cases, writers were cast in the role of literal mediators. Martha Weber physically traveled across departmental lines as a thinking, writing, speaking, and training appendage to the software that carried her trade association's database. As she explained,

> I am the administrator of the software, and I cross all departments. I write training materials for the front-end user so they can understand what they're seeing on the screen, and I can translate it to the back-end person so they can write a report. I can work with the [information technology] person and make sure there is data integrity there, and then, we can put the report with the front-end training material, merge them together, and give a complete process for someone.

Ghostwriting was another example of direct mediational work, in which individuals wrote on behalf of, and often in the persona of, other individuals, usually superiors, sometimes from previously prepared drafts and sometimes from scratch. "I do a lot of writing for other people," said development director Pam Collins. "It's difficult to put yourself in that position, you almost have to think like they think. Okay, this is a medical director writing this letter. How would a medical director write this letter?" Karen McWhorley, a young, law-school–educated, self-described "geek," writes for the signature of her firm's president, who also happens to be her father. As she explained,

> He's just an old country boy, coffee pot's always on type. There are a lot of people who are familiar with that type of personality, and they're comfortable with it. When [my father] is writing to new customers or past customers, it's part of his charm, so that has to come through. Do I use his style? No. But I make sure his personality comes out.

For others, however, the mediational work was more elaborate and abstract, as the writers themselves served as the site at which company needs and interests were transformed into tangible and transactional (written) form. Witte (2005) provides one of the fullest theoretical accounts of writing as mediation. Analyzing the work of speed bumps as mediational means to gain insight into the way that literacy functions within work activity, Witte observes that physical human actions and/or human language converge through radical transformations into nonhuman materiality. Although Witte separates mediational means (that is, material and symbolic entities) from participants (that is, human beings) and tends to emphasize the role of tools in achieving these transformations, he does recognize that from certain perspectives, writers themselves function as mediational means for others. This captures the process by which literacy serves the needs of a knowledge economy, as writers function as toolmaking tools. Indeed, from a production perspective, the mediational work of writing becomes quite pronounced, as it did in the experiential accounts of the writers I interviewed.

For instance, insurance underwriter Jacob Herron talked about the "fine line" he walked in writing health insurance policies that met the needs and requirements of multiple interests. He learned to read information coming from actuaries and legal affairs representatives as well as information he gleaned from other states and agencies to interpret and respond to health mandates. As he explained,

> There were always state statutes being amended pertaining to health law. We were breaking the law, not in compliance, unless I got these changed. You had to stay within the law. I was responsible in my states to see that I was protecting the company. And actually, you want to give the policyholders as much benefits as you can because if you don't, they go someplace else. So it impacts the sales. It's a fine line, but I dare say I got pretty good at it after awhile.

As director of marketing and corporate communications and chief all-around writer for a small bioscience company, Roxanne Richards stands between the scientists in the genetic laboratory and an array of other agents, including investors, business partners, doctors, hospital administrators, distributors, and sales representatives. Her job, as she sees it, is to communicate the "commercial essence" of "invisible" discoveries made from a science that "is abstract, new, and changing so quickly" and do it in a language that satisfies the Food and Drug Administration's (FDA) requirements for verification and disclosure. She spends a lot of time in meetings with scientists and at trade shows listening and observing with the aim of condensing technical information, human needs, and competitive pressure into a single, powerful product theme. In discussing the challenges of her work, Richards observed the following:

> People are often not willing to give writers the time and the explanation and the information necessary to really put together a

good piece. People want to throw stuff at writers in corporations and say "now do it." I find it really hard to write about something I don't feel comfortable with. And the only way you can get comfortable with it is to get intimately involved in it. Here, the science is so abstract. It's a good thing I have a strong imagination.

Ed Halloran, educational materials designer for a credit union, spoke repeatedly of a consistent institutional voice that he tried to maintain in the materials he designed, wrote, or edited—a voice that would keep the materials linked to the history and values of American cooperatives. He found what he called this inclusive voice sometimes in conflict with the third-person voice of the expert, the educator, which dominated the educational materials, as well as the voice of the "bean counters, the business people." Yet Halloran said preserving that voice and passing it on through the instructional materials was "one of the principles I set for myself in any project."

These testimonies illuminate how literacy as a human skill is recruited as an instrument of production in the knowledge economy. If machines amalgamate and transform material inputs into products for transaction, these workplace writers undertake similar processes but with much more abstract and intangible inputs. Through intense mediation, founded on processes of reading and writing, they bring coherence and shape (in the form of texts) to the disparate processes, interests, histories, goals, and needs of an organization. That this manufacturing process occurs as mental and scribal activity, that production relies so closely on the consciousness, language, values, and judgment of individual writers, is something to notice. I found it telling that the word *integrity* appeared so frequently in these writers' accounts, referring interchangeably to the integrity of their organizations or professions, the formal integrity of texts, and the personal integrity of the writers themselves. In any case, mediation and synthesis speak to what can be most intense, most difficult, most satisfying, and ultimately most exploitative about workplace writing, as powerful institutional, economic, and regulatory forces mix with the heart and brain of the writer. Mediation and synthesis, always at the core of composition and its technologies, are principal processes by which the powers of literacy are now being put under the control of economic production.

Writing and Regulation

People who write for a living find their work defined by the deepening role of codified knowledge in economic productivity and the deepening role of texts in economic exchange and competition. In the knowledge economy, manufacturing writing comes to the center of organizational concern. Great expenditures of time, money, space, and human effort are now devoted to the management of communication and the production and maintenance of textual quality. As texts become the chief vehicles for economic transactions and the chief grounds for making profits or achieving advantage, they also become potential vehicles for expensive error, impropriety, and even crime. It is not surprising that rules and regulatory agents have a growing presence in the oversight of writing (and its writers).

The history of the regulation of writing by federal and state government as well as professional licensing organizations is beyond the scope of this chapter. Suffice it to say that even among this small group of twelve workplace writers, regulatory intervention was dramatic and consequential. The interviews were peppered with references to such overseers as the FDA, the Securities and Exchange Commission (SEC), the National Association of Securities Dealers (NASD), the Health and Life Compliance Association, the National Credit Union Association, the State Insurance Commission, the Federal Housing Administration, the Department of Financial Institutions, and the Internal Revenue Service, among others. Many of the writers I interviewed consulted with in-house lawyers in the course of writing texts. Several worked in industries so highly regulated that every text produced in the firm was considered a regulated document, requiring formal protocols in the handling of it. For a great many of these writers, regulations pertaining to their industries were in a constant state of change, requiring ongoing work on their part, ranging from researching the changes to interpreting their significance to communicating that significance to others to rewriting texts to maintain compliance. In the case of insurance worker Jacob Herron, escalating government mandates pertaining to policyholder privacy and provision of benefits forced him out of underwriting and into full-time oversight of enforcement compliance and eventually into lobbying efforts on behalf of his insurance company.

In addition to creating work, regulations influenced what could be written. They sometimes put whole topics off limits. For instance, Martha Weber reported that her distance education department decided not to develop instructional materials dealing with investment policy, despite its relevance to many of her constituents. "It was too touchy," she said. "I came from a mutual fund company and knew all those issues, and I said, guys, you are going places you just don't want to go." As an educational materials designer for a financial cooperative, Ed Halloran saw deregulation enter his industry in the 1980s, and then, following national savings and loans scandals, he saw regulation return in the 1990s. He said certain educational topics in fast-changing areas were left alone by his book development department because the changes threatened to make training materials obsolete before enough copies could be sold.

Other writers I interviewed experienced regulation closer to the composition process itself. To be in compliance with plain English mandates from his state insurance commission, underwriter Jacob Herron used to mail drafts of his insurance policies to a local free-lancer who would measure his writing with the Rudolph Flesch readability formula. Martha Weber also said readability formulas were "taken to heart" in her department. "You couldn't use words with more than three syllables. You couldn't have sentences longer than eight or nine words," she explained.

As a member of one of the most regulated industries in the country, securities dealer George Carlisle reported extremely specific language regulations mandated by the SEC and enforced by the NASD. Noting that "there are things that you just don't say to people," he elaborated by saying the following:

> I'm regulated by the NASD. So there are standards set forth. If a product is offered by a prospectus, which is a legal description, you can't make qualitative comments about the product in a letter because it would reflect on the prospectus. You can't underline or reference pages in the prospectus. It falls outside the rules and regulations.

Roxanne Richards also reported writing under stiff constraints in her work, first with a medical device company and later with a genetics research firm. Recalling the previous position, she explained, "We had to work hand in hand with the regulatory affairs people. It's mandated by the FDA that the last person to see a regulated document in a corporation has to be the regulatory officer." Martha Weber, whose trade association sold tens of thousands of copies of training materials nationwide, said the last stage in production involved "the compliance and legal issues. Our lawyers have to read everything."

For the most part, the writers I spoke with appreciated the need for regulation. Of the FDA audits, registered nurse Pam Collins remarked that "you wanted to be very careful that you didn't put anybody at undue risk" and said that she "internalized respect for those regulations." However, some people I interviewed could chafe under the restrictions. As securities dealer Carlisle observed:

> We're dealing with people's money, their future, their retirement, their children's education. Better to be overregulated than

underregulated. [But] some of the new regulations have made it difficult to properly educate people because of what you can do and can't do in print.

To sum up, federal regulatory agencies or their surrogates have direct influence on the manufacturing of texts in a number of different fields in ways that can create work for writers; control their language; engage them in direct surveillance, either as objects or agents; and influence their sense of efficacy. Along with elements of mediation, the influence of regulation coursing through the composition process is a mark of contemporary workplace writing for many individuals. A later section will consider some of the implications of these pressures.

Demands for Change

Another hallmark feature of the knowledge economy is the pace of change within it. Because the knowledge economy requires new knowledge for growth, a high premium is placed on innovation along with a drive for greater efficiency and expanding markets (Boisot, 1999; Neef, 1998; Zack, 1999). The search for what is different, faster, smarter, and more effectively communicated and sold drives economic activity at an unprecedented pitch and introduces the potential for rapid and continuous change in the workplace. Indeed, that the quest for economic advantage in knowledge-producing fields relies so deeply on human ingenuity, skills, and effort can make the modern workplace a challenging, turbulent, and often unstable environment.

Earlier, I mentioned how many of the people I interviewed saw their job titles and even careers shifting, often in response to competitive changes in science, law, financial climates, and technology. Although still in her twenties, mortgage broker Karen McWhorley already had moved from the human resources department of her father's larger firm to start up and dissolve several small companies in response to shifts in mortgage rates and regulatory practices in the banking and lending industry. Trade association executive Martha Weber took a quantum leap in 1999 into software management in part as a response to the Y2K crisis. A week before I interviewed him, Jacob Herron took early retirement from an insurance company that had phased out his entire unit in an efficiency move. In the summer of 2004, fifty-four-year-old Ed Halloran was seeing his position as an educational materials designer completely redefined as the decision was made to move all training activity completely online. And George Carlisle, senior manager of an investment firm who had relied for years on giving dictation to an assistant, had recently enrolled in a typing class at a local community college so that he could free up his assistant to do more writing and interpretative work. Although much is made of the effect of change on members affiliated with the older, manufacturing economies, knowledge-intensive work itself is in the eye of the storm, creating instability and turbulence for those who write and intensifying demand on the resilience of literate ability. As I will demonstrate later, career and work cause changes not only in the distribution of skills but also in the distribution of the very opportunities one has for writing as well as the particular genres with which one engages. Furthermore, as these changes radiate into the society at large, they affect writers' rhetorical conditions, including the knowledge environments in which they work and the shifting habits of readers they must reach.

Change was ubiquitous and was ubiquitously recognized among those I interviewed. As Martha Weber remarked, "What I was doing in the 1980s in distance education was very antiquated when you look back at it. Today, distance education is fully automated; the students get immediate feedback." In discussing her attempt to keep up with legal conditions in the area of artificial reproduction, attorney Lauren Bickle observed that "this is a case where the science is ahead of the law." Regarding the investment industry during the past decade,

George Carlisle observed that "I had a great picture of a dam with floodgates." Change also registered in the intense level of training and retraining that the interviewees reported. As pivotal producers in the knowledge economy, members of the writing class generally find their literacy and overall efficacy a site of ongoing investment by their employers. Except for those who were self-employed, everyone I interviewed had attended work-related training, ranging from several weeks at special institutes to day-long in-house classes. In addition, several pursued self-education via career-related reading during leisure hours.

Although changes of all kinds influenced how these writers did their work, I will confine myself in this section to considering how reading and writing were affected most directly and how the interviewees themselves adjusted their understanding of reading and writing as a result of changes in the workplace. For instance, restructuring in Jacob Herron's corporation had brought the emergence of large project teams, which often oversaw the planning and review of written reports, making composing, in Herron's view, less individually motivated and controlled, less efficient, and less satisfying. Increased work and less time also affected the kinds of writing Herron was able to produce. He stopped writing feature-length articles on health issues for his company's in-house magazine, a monthly pleasure he used to take. He also said the pace of change and the emergence of e-mail had turned him into "a stenographer," with no time to write the "beautiful three- and four-page health memos" that he used to write. Other older workers reported changes to their writing in response to the demand for speed and the growing reliance on the Internet for routine communication. Securities dealer George Carlisle, who had to learn how to type in his mid-fifties, said the reliance on technology for interoffice communication was impersonal and prevented him "from reading the person. You can't do that over the Internet." He also remarked that e-mail brought "unwanted permanency" to some forms of communication. Martha Weber discussed being pushed to write in increasingly brief, precise, and uncluttered ways to satisfy busy managers. Ed Halloran, who talked about "a whole culture that now revolves around the computer rather than typed words on paper," remarked on the significant transition he was making from book form to online form in the instructional materials under development in his department:

> I have to learn how to write in different ways and formats that are brief and to the point and organized in shorter paragraphs and in shorter sentences with simpler words. Where once we would bring in a manuscript of thirty thousand words, working in PowerPoint, we are down to five hundred characters per screen. So it's stepping down by magnitudes the information we can convey. That's communication nowadays.

These testimonies demonstrate how adaptability in the contemporary workplace includes in part an ability to respond to changes in the conditions for writing (including arrangements of time, space, and participants), changes in genres (such that experiences developed through one genre may be lost to or at least transformed by the demands of the new), as well as changes in available means for the treatment of others through writing (as new media presume or enact different interactive relationships). These testimonies also illuminate how the knowledge economy is developing a deep interest in the literacy practices not only of producers but also of the consumers of writing. How the economy works is now deeply entangled in how people read and write, making the pressures for changes around literacy unlikely to abate.

Literacy and the Knowledge Economy

In *Measuring What People Know: Human Capital Accounting for the Knowledge Economy,* the Organization for Economic Cooperation and Development (1996) discusses the slippery issues involved in aligning human capital with accounting procedures that have traditionally applied to land, machines, and money. Indeed, much business and government theorizing now goes into figuring out how to assess the worth of knowledge-reliant industries (Becker, 1994; Boisot, 1999; Stewart, 1997). The conceptual difficulties are many, especially because knowledge, as Burton-Jones (1999) puts it, is "leaky property" (p. 225). When the assets are human, companies cannot own them, but they can grow them and try to control them. Literacy in the twenty-first century will be inevitably influenced by these forces.

Growing knowledge is why training and learning are so important to the new economy. Furthermore, in the knowledge economy, learning is regarded as a basic task of production and a part of what is created at every stage of production so that new knowledge can be cycled back into the production process (Nevis, DiBella, and Gould, 2000). The concern is to organize knowledge flows in workplaces so that people inside companies can communicate with each other more regularly and teach each other more easily. At the same time, knowledge must be protected and even obscured to maintain a competitive edge. The aim is to embed knowledge deeply within organizational routines and structures so that it does not belong to any one person. There are attempts to identify the core competencies of a corporation so that they can be rearranged to invent new products and, most important, be preserved during periods of layoffs (Cross and Israelit, 2000; Prahalad and Hamel, 1999). Attention is paid to just-in-time strategic learning. And there are lots of models for sharing intelligence between people and technology as well as skimming off, codifying, leveraging, or organizing the cognitive assets of individuals into collective resources, what several people I interviewed referred to as "skill sets" (Cohen and Levinthal, 2000).

The testimonies of the twelve writers I interviewed suggest how literacy as human capital is caught up in this process, affecting the way that workplace writers encounter the rhythms of learning, competition, and regulation that mark the making, buying, and sell-ing of knowledge. Several of the people I interviewed, notably the insurance executive, the educational materials designer, and the mort-gage broker, found how they wrote and what they wrote affected by major restructurings either in their individual corporations or in their industries more widely. For Jacob Herron, the creation of proj-ect teams in his insurance company forced on him a collective writing process in which he lost much of his earlier autonomy. The mortgage broker Karen McWhorley, who depended heavily on her own knowl-edge of the lending industry and an ability to make the right written connections with far-flung banking officials and customers, could see her effectiveness suddenly restructured by a new lending law or even a new lending rate. At the time of our interview, educational materials designer Ed Halloran was involved in a complete overhaul of the pro-duction of educational materials from books to online formats, a jolt, he acknowledged, to his "linear approach to information and commu-nication." These cases demonstrate that literacy can be implicated in so many dimensions of restructuring, from the social context of com-posing to the grounds on which competition is waged to the forms of written product themselves.

At the same time that knowledge companies cultivate core compe-tencies, knowledge remains a "leaky property," meaning that "human assets" inside companies can carry their learning (including their lit-eracy learning) into other contexts and projects of self-development. And they do. As Roxanne Richardson put it, "if you write, you learn." This learning often traveled beyond the workplace. Accountant Barry Freund said he often found information he researched for custom-ers coming in handy in his own life, an experience also reported by business magazine editor David Dubrowsky. Securities dealer George Carlisle said he and his college-age son had become quite adept at money management. Martha Weber wrote letters and training manuals for the small business owned by her husband. Ed Halloran served as the editor for books written by his retired father. Several people also reported getting recruited for writing tasks within social and civic organizations to which they belonged. "People tend to say, oh, you're a lawyer, you're a good writer," said Lauren Bickle.

The social capital of literacy and knowledge that travels beyond the workplace and into family and social relations would not be accounted for in any spreadsheet. Nor would the value and satisfaction of authorship, which was widely expressed among the people I interviewed. These individuals worked in places where authorship was widely distributed, where acts could be made permanent through the written word, and where the words and deeds of these writers could be amplified by the great resources of the workplace, albeit sometimes in anonymity. Wracked at times by being in the "crass business of using high art for low purposes," marketing director Roxanne Richards nevertheless took satisfaction in having a hand in promoting genetic research: "It is something you can feel good about because in ten or twenty years, it's going to have a positive impact on whether someone lives or dies." Attorney Lauren Bickle talked with great satisfaction about a phrase she coined for an appeals case that was reiterated by the judge in his ruling and then picked up and used (although not attributed to her) all over the country, eventually making its way into some of the magazines she reads on adoption and family law: "My name isn't on it or anything, but I did write it." Accountant Barry Freund spoke about how responding to the needs of audiences is a source of intellectual challenge and satisfaction. "The writing that you do makes you think," he observed. "If you really try to put yourself in somebody else's shoes, it gives you a different outlook on things." Earlier, I mentioned how educational materials designer Ed Halloran took particular satisfaction in creating a voice in corporate documents that aligned closely with his political values. He also found the resources of his workplace, including the time, space, and relative autonomy afforded him, presented opportunities for good works, including, most recently, aiding in fundraising for a new secondary school in East Africa. Of his nonprofit financial institution, he said that

> It's an environment that encourages us to participate. We do work in eighty different countries, so I'm exposed to international projects, not so much directly on my job, but I go to training events or informational events and meet people from other countries.

Out of one of these contacts, Halloran was asked to write the school's fundraising prospectus, and he continues to assist the school founders with their communication needs. Mass access to authorship is a relatively new phenomenon in the history of literacy, thanks in no small part to changes in work. How this identity is worn and carried through the society is a chapter still unfolding.

At the same time, it must be remembered that such authorship is forged as forms of labor and in contexts of competition and control. In the knowledge economy, human development, including literacy development, is increasingly embedded in product development. Where in the production process one stands determines the forms of reading and writing one undertakes, and there was plenty of evidence in the interviews of the ingraining of literate patterns through habits of work. Jacob Herron took great pride in having successfully internalized the Flesch formula of readability, which is required by many state insurance commissions: "I always would pass whatever it had to be. You learn to write the same language no matter what state it is for." "Work continues to make me very left brain," software manager Martha Weber observed, as she described applying "process analysis" to everyday tasks beyond work. "The process is just so ingrained." And securities dealer George Carlisle, a former history teacher now "licensed to read" all documents in and out of his investment firm for regulatory violations, said, "Even when I read for pleasure, which I don't do enough of, I find myself reading just for the high points. Just the way I read e-mails. I seldom sit down and just let the book take me."

Government analysts continue to ponder the costs and benefits of human assets, including literacy, in the knowledge economy. However, the costs and benefits to humans have been much less explored. This chapter has offered one gesture in the latter direction. The knowledge economy presents both potentials and problems for the future of literacy. On the one hand, through the interviews, I could see enormous investments in human development going on in many of these workplaces, at least in the stratum investigated here. People who write for a living find access to teaching, learning, information, time, and space as well as powerful systems of communication, organization, and legitimacy, all of which give rise, in many cases, to challenging and stimulating work, self-growth, self-esteem, monetary reward, and opportunities to share resources with others. On the other hand, these opportunities for writing, learning, and sharing are configured not necessarily in terms of the worth or rights of the individual under development but rather in rationales of production and profit making. The capture of literacy for economic production and competition introduces great demand and support for writing, yet also great instability and turbulence into workplace writing practices. People who write for a living must function under these conditions often as intense mediators of powerful ideological processes, mingling self and system as they transform abstract need into transactional texts. Furthermore, the knowledge economy also is giving rise to more regulation around the written word on the part of government, the same entity charged with protecting free speech. These conflicts and contradictions, which matter in the lives of those who write and matter to the destiny of literacy itself, deserve more investigation and debate not only by literacy scholars but also by writers and citizens everywhere.

References

Bazerman, C. *The Languages of Edison's Light.* Cambridge, Mass.: MIT Press, 2002.

Becker, G. S. *Human Capital.* (3rd ed.) Chicago: University of Chicago Press, 1994.

Beniger, J. F. *The Control Revolution: Technological and Economic Origins of the Information Society.* Cambridge, Mass.: Harvard University Press, 1986.

Boisot, M. H. *Knowledge Assets: Securing Competitive Advantage in the Information Economy.* New York: Oxford University Press, 1999.

Brandt, D. *Reading, Writing and Wealth.* (Speaker Series No. 21.) Minneapolis: University of Minnesota Center for the Interdisciplinary Study of Writing, 2002.

Burton-Jones, A. *Knowledge Capitalism: Business, Work and Learning in the New Economy.* New York: Oxford University Press, 1999.

Castells, M. *The Informational City: Information Technology, Economic Restructuring and the Urban-Regional Process.* Cambridge, Mass.: Blackwell, 1989.

Cohen, W. M., and Levinthal, D. A. "Absorptive Capacity: A New Perspective on Learning and Innovation." In R. Cross and S. Israelit (eds.), *Strategic Learning in a Knowledge Economy: Individual, Collective and Organizational Learning Process* (pp. 39–67). Boston: Butterworth-Heinemann, 2000.

Cross, G. A. *Collaboration and Conflict: A Contextual Exploration of Group Writing and Positive Emphasis.* Cresskill, N.J.: Hamptom, 1993.

Cross, R., and Israelit, S. (eds.). *Strategic Learning in a Knowledge Economy: Individual, Collective and Organizational Learning Process.* Boston: Butterworth-Heinemann, 2000.

Drucker, P. F. *Post-Capitalist Society.* New York: Harper, 1994.

Florida, R. *The Rise of the Creative Class.* New York: Perseus, 2002.

Lay, M. M., and Karis, W. M. *Collaborative Writing in Industry.* Amity, N.Y.: Baywood, 1991.

Lunsford, A., and Ede, L. *Singular Texts/Plural Authors: Perspectives on Collaborative Writing.* Carbondale: Southern Illinois University Press, 1990.

Neef, D. (ed.). *The Knowledge Economy.* Boston: Butterworth-Heinemann, 1998.

Nevis, E. C., DiBella, A. J., and Gould, J. M. "Understanding Organizations as Learning Systems." In R. Cross and S. Israelit (eds.), *Strategic Learning in a Knowledge Economy: Individual, Collective and Organizational Learning Process* (pp. 119–140). Boston: Butterworth-Heinemann, 2000.

Organization for Economic Cooperation and Development (OECD). *Measuring What People Know: Human Capital Accounting for the Knowledge Economy.* Paris: OECD, 1996.

Prahalad, C. K., and Hamel, G. "The Core Competence of the Corporation." In M. H. Zack (ed.), *Knowledge and Strategy* (pp. 41–59). Boston: Butterworth-Heinemann, 1999.

Romer, P. *Human Capital and Growth.* Washington, D.C.: Bureau of Economic Research, 1989.

Scribner, S., and Cole, M. *The Psychology of Literacy.* Cambridge, Mass.: Harvard University Press, 1981.

Stewart, T. A. *Intellectual Capital: The New Wealth of Organizations.* New York: Doubleday, 1997.

Strauss, A. L. *Qualitative Analysis for Social Scientists.* New York: Cambridge University Press, 1987.

Strauss, A. L., and Corbin, J. M. *Basics of Qualitative Research: Techniques and Procedures for Developing Grounded Theory.* Thousand Oaks, Calif.: Sage, 1998.

Street, B. *Social Literacies: Critical Approaches to Literacy Development, Ethnography and Education.* New York: Addison-Wesley, 1995.

Witte, S. P. "Research in Activity: An Analysis of Speed Bumps as Mediational Means." *Written Communication,* 2005, *22*, 127–165.

Zack, M. H. (ed.) *Knowledge and Strategy.* Boston: Butterworth-Heinemann, 1999.

6

The Status of Writing

A PROMINENT EAST COAST VANITY PRESS ANNOUNCED RECENTLY that it was the first ghostwriting firm in the country to offer their clients insurance protection against charges of plagiarism. Yes, for an extra fee people who pay other people to write books for which they will take the credit are protected in the event that the people they hire are using somebody else's work without crediting it. In announcing this new line of service, the press release warned of the dire consequences of the charge of plagiarism, including "major lawsuits, financial ruin, a destroyed reputation, and a lifetime of stigma" and went on to assert: "The best way to safeguard yourself against plagiarism is to work with a reputable ghostwriting firm."[1]

We might dismiss the offer of plagiarism insurance as a cynical ploy: one that excites anxiety while pretending to quell anxiety about the recent spate of plagiarism cases against well-known authors and scholars while also muddling the already muddled lines of personal responsibility. But I would like to suggest that this announcement brings into focus some of the unusual and often convoluted dynamics in the status of writing, dynamics that too often remain muted in our research and teaching. Writing is unique among the so-called language arts because of its direct role in the creation of economic wealth, a role that has only intensified over the last fifty years as our economy (and our literacy) have been reconfigured for the production of information and knowledge. Written texts are bought and sold, and writing has legal and social standing as a form of labor (Angel and Tannebaum, 1976–77; Burk, 2004; Smart, 2008). In contexts of production, competition and profit, the writing act can be broken down, like a manufacturing process, mapped onto hierarchies of power and material ownership, used, in some cases, for the execution of deception or crime, and exploited for every ounce of value, including symbolic value, that accrues to it (Burton-Jones, 1999; Prahalad and Hamel, 1999; Stewart, 1997). At the vanity press, for instance, there is a sliding scale for hiring ghostwriters. If you want a ghostwriter who has worked for the *New York Times,* you pay more for that prestigious association, just as ghostwriters can earn higher fees and bragging rights if their work comes out under the byline of a celebrity or other high-value person.

It is this transactional or fungible quality of writing—the way it is amenable to systems of work, wage, and market—that gives writing its unusual status in the history of mass literacy and makes it so different from reading. Reading obviously plays a role in generating and sharing information or knowledge (not to mention a role in generating and transacting writing itself), and reading can be a source of great symbolic or cultural capital. Yet reading is not fungible like writing and usually cannot participate unadulterated in systems of exchange in the same way as writing. Nor is reading in and of itself recognized legally as a form of labor (even though it clearly often is). Reading as a process or a product has little value until it is transacted—most often, in the form of writing.

Throughout most of its history, reading has participated in a different kind of economy from writing, what Harvey Graff refers to as a moral economy (1979, p. 26). The value of reading at least until now has rested in its ability to inculcate shared beliefs, values, tastes, identities. Reading from the perspective of those who have sponsored it and those who learn it has been for the production or maintenance of right thinking, assimilation, further learning, discovery, edification or pleasure (also see Kaestle, 1983; Soltow and Stevens, 1981). Reading contributes something to the reader. It is for good but it is not a good. You might be enriched by reading the great American novel but to get rich you will have to write one—or look up a reputable ghostwriting firm.

What interests me about the case of the plagiarism insurance, however, is that it demonstrates how much the commercial value of writing is nested within the moral economy of reading, a relationship that ghostwriting depends upon even as it seems to undermine it. Writers gain stature in part because of the good that they do—they contribute to the moral and intellectual growth of readers. Because many forms of reading over time have been marked with high cultural value, this value has come to extend to those who can write in those forms. When ghostwriters sell authorship rights, they transfer that moral stature to their paying clients. So the economy of reading makes the commercial prospects of ghostwriting good, but the economy of reading also shapes the ethical expectations that make plagiarism bad.[2] Plagiarism is a form of material theft but what makes it so morally egregious is that it betrays the trust fundamental to the act of reading; it interrupts the moral transfer of the good from writer to reader. Plagiarism victimizes readers by making them unwitting receivers of stolen goods, dampening prospects of moral uplift that reading usually promises. So plagiarism insurance (a commodity positioned squarely, even ingeniously, in the economy of writing) serves as a commercial solution to a moral dilemma—a chance for the author to re-separate if conditions warrant from the moral responsibility of authorship and claim victimization along with readers. The case of plagiarism insurance puts the commercial economy of writing on a collision course with the moral economy of reading—a trend that I want to suggest is becoming more common as mass writing continues to grow in economic and cultural power and to eclipse reading as the literate practice of consequence. As writing ascends in importance, it could displace if not undo the moral arrangements of reading, at least as they have been understood until now.

In the history of mass literacy, reading and writing have developed in radically different ways in terms of the cultural and economic forces that have sponsored and sanctioned them as well as the social rationales through which they have been taken up (Furet and Ozouf, 1983). Although these days reading and writing are typically taught together in school, studied together, and treated as similar underlying or mutually dependent processes, their different cultural origins remain consequential to the ways that they are accessed, practiced, and experienced as part of ordinary life.[3] It is in fact the radical difference between writing and reading that must be better apprehended in order to understand mass literacy as it is going forward. In the older, moral regime of literacy, readers were presumed to be many and writers were presumed to be few. But with recent economic, social and technological changes, writing is coming to rival reading as a condition of mass literate experience. Writers are becoming many. In these circumstances, the real differences between writing and reading are erupting. The radically different social rationales and sponsorship networks of writing are coming into prominence. The surge in writing has the potential to alter long standing assumptions and values that surround literacy as a whole and to put new pressures on social institutions that have been built around the moral economy of reading. When we laugh at the idea of plagiarism insurance, we feel these pressures close by.

Mass reading emerged gradually in the United States through the eighteenth and nineteenth century largely through the sponsoring agents of church and state. Reading was critical to salvation in the ideology of the Protestant church and to citizenship in the ideology of the Republic (Brown, 1996; Gilmore, 1989; Graff, 1995). In the initial project of mass literacy, however, writing held no great sway. Harder to teach, messy to learn, not as suitable a vehicle for religious or social control, and especially dangerous in the hands of the oppressed, mass writing emerged separately from mass reading and more slowly through the eighteenth and nineteenth centuries (Cornelius, 1991; Kaestle, 1983; Monaghan, 2005; Williams, 2005). It was promulgated not through church and state but through artisanship and commerce (Long, 2001; Longo, 2000; Stevens, 1995). Those who wrote depended on patrons with power and money to subsidize their efforts (Amory and Hall, 2007; Finkelstein, 2008). First linked not with worship but with work, not with reading but with mathematics and accounting, writing was rarely central to doctrines of salvation or assimilation and has been far less promoted or sanctioned by the state. The association of writing with the practical world of commerce, craft, and mercantilism helps to explain why writing instruction in colonial America was largely excluded from the literacy campaigns of churches and Sunday schools as well as from the traditional grammar school. Writing was taught instead in separate, private-pay settings and found its value in the budding communication trades and service economy of the new nation. Over time, writing continued to be the vehicle by which rising levels of literacy could be claimed for economic competition and productivity. This legacy continues to organize relationships between reading and writing in ways that matter to everyday Americans and their literacy.

In what follows I want to continue to explore the collision between the moral economy of reading and the commercial economy of writing, a collision that challenges social institutions that have grown up around the older regime of a reading literacy and, like our opening example, pose perplexing questions about how mass literacy will go forward. I will be drawing on a research project in progress in which I am conducting in-depth interviews with people caught up in writing intensity, either at work or in elective time, in various occupations and life circumstances. In the interviews, we explore the kinds of writing they do, how they learned how to do it, and how it influences their other experiences with literacy. I draw here from the initial phase of the research, which focused on middle-class workers in professional, administrative, and technical occupations, people who have had at least two years of postsecondary education. In analyzing their interviews, I sought patterns that could articulate a rivalry between writing and reading, particularly as it sets up potential contradictions in the meanings and value of literacy. Here I characterize those key patterns and explore their significance.

Writing has more direct transactional value than reading. The commercial claim over writing has had many implications for the reading-writing relationship but above all it has meant that private enterprise has always invested heavily in the support of writing, shaping opportunities for learning and intervening into writing processes in ways with no readily apparent equivalent on the reading side. These investments and interventions have only intensified as the economy has shifted to the broad-based manufacturing of information and knowledge. This shift put written texts and the skills that fuel them at the center of production and quality control. One can see these investments in the physical arrangements of contemporary workplaces. Over the past few years I have visited, for example, a large insurance building with an entire, secure floor designated for writing policies; a police station with a so-called quiet room for writing reports; a law firm with a soundproof, windowless room for writing briefs. There are temporal arrangements as well. One stockbroker and his staff wrote proposals in what he called "power blocks" of time, four and five hour stretches in a day set aside for what he called "big time writing" when, he said, "no one gets near us." These same prerogatives are not accorded to reading unless it is embedded in the production or oversight of writing. In the workplace, reading does not enjoy big-time status; no four or five hours of the work day devoted only to reading. In fact, significant professional reading often goes on during private hours, off the clock, in the evening or on weekends or during travel or waiting time.

Nor does reading seem to be tested or taught in the workplace in the same direct way that writing is. In fact, the explicit teaching of writing in the workplace—whether peer to peer or supervisor to supervised or in workshops and seminars—has been one of the most eye-opening aspects of my current investigations into workplace writing. The subsidies surrounding writing in terms of money, personnel, time, and technology are staggering, as are the levels of intervention. Some of these interventions have a familiar, school-like quality to them. Consider this memory from a current software developer whose first job was with a public radio station in the 1980s:

> I was a kid, nineteen years old, and my writing was terrible but they beat me into good writing and you know I hated being told you know this stinks, write it again. Or just having red scribbles all over the stuff. But the people who mentored me were really good and made me into an acceptable writer through a lot of pain. I would submit something that took me an hour to write. They would tear it apart in ten seconds and say do it again. And through this iterative process I got better. I hated it, but it was really valuable.

In the following brief testimonies—which are provided by supervisors from an array of settings—we can see how pedagogical intervention into employees' language styles and writing processes fits seamlessly into their duties of leadership and oversight. The interventions are justified—almost without saying—by the high stakes that surround corporate communication and written products. Notice how much explicit modeling, rhetorical training, and correction occur:

> The letter has to flow. It has to be interesting and good and an easy read. So that's what I'm teaching—what to say and what not to say.
>
> I don't use a red pen. I don't highlight. But I suggest. And it might be something like—if I were writing this I don't think I'd send this out in this form. Look at this.

It's important for me to make sure my staff understands what they can and cannot say in their correspondence with people who contact this office. So in that way I've guided them on the terminology.

I just make sure I articulate our vision and make sure they understand it. When we write, we ask, what's our outcome, what are we trying to achieve? If someone reads this, what do we want them to think? I make sure I walk people through that process.

I'll do some coaching or work with them. Something about their style may be too abrupt or that sort of thing. Just to make sure things are written in the tone that this administration will want us to be giving to the world at large.

If somebody hands me something, I would edit it or else maybe go back to their desk and say, here, I made a couple of changes. In some cases I might say, let's do it this way. It's not like I'm gathering people around me and saying here is how we're going to write, although I don't think that is a bad idea.

Reading instruction was rarely provided in the professional settings I visited, save for the occasional seminar in speed reading. When workplace reading instruction did occur, it was directed at employees in low-level positions, especially immigrants, whose problems with reading English on the job were seen to interfere with safety and efficiency. This instruction was almost always government-financed, in the form of basic education classes or ESL courses, sometimes offered at the work site but usually in other settings like community centers or community colleges. That is, even in the workplace reading instruction seems to remain associated primarily with cultural assimilation and state sponsorship. Private writing instruction and writing support took place at the higher levels, among white collar workers, on company time, and the more important the writing one did, the more support one reliably received. I interviewed an attorney, for example, whose writing was routinely supported by a flotilla of helpers: researchers, assistants who served as editors, as well as clerical staff who compensated for his (nearly total) lack of computer skills. In the workplace, writing literacy is developed, sustained, renewed, assisted and amplified as a by-product of production and within hierarchies of power that lend different values to different aspects of the work of literacy. As a result, opportunities for learning and receiving assistance (not to mention routine access to powerful communication technologies) depends on one's location in the production process. The modern workplace is a school for writing but a school without the mandates for universal literacy that grew up around the evangelizing church or the common school which, in name at least, offered to teach literacy—that is, a reading literacy—to all. Today the tightening association between socioeconomic status and literacy, the growing gaps in wealth between the literacy-haves and the literacy have-nots, stem in part from the patterns of access and investment that accompany the role of writing in economic production—an inequality between public investment in reading and private investment in writing.

The high-stakes transactional status of writing leads to a second key difference. *The government regulates writing more highly than reading.* As the materiality of writing makes it more readily transactional than reading, it also makes it more amenable to monitoring and accountability, especially by government or its surrogates. As texts have become chief vehicles for economic transaction, they also have become potential vehicles for expensive error, impropriety, and even crime. As a result, regulatory agencies have a widespread presence in the oversight of everyday writing and its writers (Himmelberg, 1994). The interviews I am having with workplace writers are peppered with references to such overseers as the Food and Drug Administration, the Securities and Exchange Commission, the National Association of Securities Dealers, the Health and Life Compliance Association, the National Credit Union Association, the State Insurance Commission, the Federal Housing Administration, the Department of Financial Institutions, among others. Many of the writers I interviewed consulted with in-house lawyers in the course of writing texts. Several worked in industries so highly regulated that each text produced in the firm, even an ordinary press release, was considered a "regulated document," requiring formal protocols in the handling of it.

I interviewed a registered nurse at an HMO who was helping to run drug trials for a major pharmaceutical company. She said:

> At least twice that I can remember we got a call that the FDA agents were coming. They'd spend a couple weeks poring over all of our records and then interrogate you. Interrogate may be a little strong, but they were serious. We had to put everything out, all of our work.

A communications director for a medical device company also wrote under the shadow of the FDA:

> We had to work hand in hand with the regulatory affairs people who have these very elaborate document control systems. The document systems are unbelievable . . . So if I was writing a brochure I had to make sure that any statements I was making in that brochure could be backed up. God forbid the FDA would come in and say show me how you prove that. I had good rapport with the technical and regulatory people. I would go to my regulatory guy if I had an idea and I'd say, "Got five minutes? Here's the idea. Are you going to let me get away with it?"

I interviewed a financial advisor who, as supervisor of his branch office, was "licensed to read" all the daily e-mail traffic that went in and out of his office to ensure both employees and customers were in compliance with NASD regulations. He spent a significant portion of his work day in such mandated surveillance, carried out with the help of a special software program that "picks up the hot spots," ranging from words associated with potential insider trading to potential sexual harassment. The financial advisor said he routinely excised jokes that circulated through e-mail as potentially too risky under the regulatory circumstances. He went on:

I'm regulated by the NASD. So there are standards set forth. There are things that you just don't say to people. This is for the good of everybody. Better to be overregulated than underregulated. As you study for the exams for this profession, you understand what the regulations are and you adapt your writing skills to them. That's not to say some days I don't throw a fit because I can't express what I need to express. . . . If I'm in doubt about what I'm writing, if I'm not sure, I get on the phone and call my compliance people.

Several people I interviewed wrote in compliance with readability formulas associated with Plain English mandates. An education specialist for a national trade association explained: "You couldn't use words with more than three syllables. You couldn't have sentences longer than eight or nine words." To be in compliance with "plain English" mandates from his state insurance commission, one underwriter told me that in pre-computer days he used to be required to mail drafts of his insurance policies to a local freelancer who would measure his writing with the Rudolph Flesch readability formula and then mail the score back to him. He said:

There is a certificate you have to file. The score goes right as part of the filings. Now our computer systems have a dealie right on them that will do this. I can compose something, hit it, and it will score it. I always can pass whatever it has to be.

It is hard to fault efforts to promote clarity in contractual language, and it is hard to fault employers trying to avoid trouble from employees' unauthorized writing. But the fact remains that everyday writers at work find regulation and surveillance penetrating deeply into their cognitive and linguistic processes in ways that are just not—and cannot—be experienced in workplace reading. There is something pretty personal about having federal agents or their surrogates look at your lab notes or your outbox not in the context of a criminal investigation but as part of everyday, routine prior constraint.

I want to suggest that we can look again to the collision between the commercial economy of writing and the moral economy of reading as a contributing factor here. As a legacy of the sponsorship of mass literacy, we (for the most part) experience strong government protection of mass reading and strong government regulation of mass writing. Where writing has been *protected* by law, it has been indirectly through the protections afforded to the reading public. From the founding of the United States, reading has been linked to the rights and duties of citizenship; it is through the rights of readers that the First Amendment has found its most secure rationales in case law (Baker, 1989; Bunker, 2001; Sunstein, 1993). Freedom of the press, a cornerstone of civil liberties, functions for the sake of readers, not writers. Even intellectual property and copyright law, for that matter, have found their rationale through the needs of readers: government provides incentives and protections for creative and intellectual work in order to insure that the minds of its citizens are nourished and replenished.

At the same time, where writing has been *regulated* by law, it also has been for the protection of the citizen-reader, only this time in the role of consumer. Government justifies regulation and oversight of written communication to protect potentially gullible or under-skilled consumers who enter into contracts or seek professional advice or must make medical or other decisions based on what they read. Writing requires an active regulatory context because reading is integral to the consumption of many goods and services. As a result, prior government restraint, an anathema in the realm of publishing, is standard practice in workplace writing. Service writers (which means most of us) do not hold ground in free speech traditions. Legislatures and courts have not—at least not yet—seriously taken up the needs of writing citizens as a central concept. In fact, I would say in court cases involving speech rights and privacy rights at work, the weak protections of mass writing and mass writers in the public domain have made it easier for courts to side (as they almost always do) with employers over employees in the private domain (Townsend and Bennett, 2003). We have few legal traditions for writing citizens except in their service to reading citizens. Many of the controversies and struggles now going on around the Internet, its freedoms and constraints, as well as the literacy practices springing up there relate to this imbalance.

So far we have considered how the interplay between a market economy for literacy and a moral economy for literacy have shaped relationships between mass writing and mass reading. In the market economy writing receives higher levels of subsidy but also higher levels of stratification and control. We also have considered how the market economy seems both to depend upon the moral economy of literacy and to undermine it. This interplay puts the value systems of writing and reading into collision with each other at a time when writing is ascending in importance. This collision challenges some of the bedrock arrangements of our social institutions that have grown up around the values of a reading literacy. In this final section, I want to consider another dynamic in this relationship: the residual power of the moral economy and how it can work to devalue writing.

Mass writing is given less ethical and moral value than mass reading. As mentioned above, for most of the history of mass literacy, the value of writing has resided in the reading of it, not the doing of it. Authorship gained its prestige from its power to morally uplift a readership. It is through the moral transactions of reading that we are thought to develop desirable attributes of character and civic mindedness (Graff, 1979). So recent reports of precipitous declines in book reading (for instance, by the National Endowment for the Arts, 2004) are bemoaned as a collapse in democracy and civilization—even as those same reports acknowledge a sharp uptick in writing among ordinary Americans. While literary reading is down, down, down, literary writing is up, up, up some 30 percent over the last NEA survey in 1992. Creative writing is especially popular among the group doing the least amount of reading, the young.

That the NEA fails to extol, let along explain, this significant shift in literacy activity away from reading and toward writing speaks, I think, to the general cultural difficulty of incorporating writing into a moral vision of literacy, particularly writing that seems so unanchored in or untrained by the discipline of reading. Writing as a rival to reading as a site of character formation has very little presence so far in the official history of mass literacy. We have few stories in our culture of anyone writing themselves into a divine or morally improved condition. If reading makes us more informed, independent, innovative, productive and free, what does writing do—except apparently make us less inclined to read?

Yet in talking to workaday writers, I have been struck by their frequent reports of intense aesthetic experience, heightened awareness of language, deep ethical sensibility, and the pleasures they derive from what can only be called authorship, including the satisfaction of feeling their words enter and at times alter the environments that surround them. Economic and technological changes over the last forty years have been making conditions for authorship available on an unprecedented scale. These conditions include organizational time and space for composing; routine access to powerful communication technologies; connections to audiences; complex problems to which writing is being addressed; and high stakes around the solutions to those problems. While this writing is commercial or bureaucratic, it does place individual writers into intense intellectual and communicative dramas out of which aesthetic and civic experiences—along with, of course, frustration, exhaustion, and other emotive experiences—derive. So used are we to viewing reading as the first and fundamental skill in literacy, so ingrained is the idea that the capacity to write well depends on the capacity to read well, that it is hard to imagine a future in which writing might precede or precipitate or support reading or compete with it for people's attentions and energies. But that future is upon us.

Several people that I interviewed, for instance, made analogies to the arts in describing their workplace writing, highlighting inventiveness and perspective taking often associated with painting, sculpting, filmmaking, fiction writing. I talked with a policy analyst whose job it is to whittle down huge amounts of data into action documents for a cabinet secretary, who sometimes will have only two minutes or less to attend to the analyst's digest. He said: "For me, it's almost like sculpting. That's essentially the skill I think I have."

I interviewed a freelance writer who, among other things, ghostwrote personal newsletter columns for CEOs in the banking industry. Her analogy was to film: "I got comfortable in that producer-director role. The star is someone else. So what you are doing is script writing. They are Tom Hanks and you are Steven Spielberg or Dorothy Parker would be my preferred role model."

And another ghostwriter I interviewed likened his jump into the mind of his boss to taking on another persona. He said: "It's like acting. I think it is a challenge to be somebody different from you but you aren't really becoming that person. You just try to stand in that person's shoes."

Many people I interviewed wrote narrative reports involving figures to whom they felt great responsibility and whose lives they wanted to represent in full dimension. I talked with an intake social worker at a drug unit at a veteran's hospital. She interviews clients and writes narratives about them that guide decisions of physicians, psychiatrists, lawyers, and parole officers. We can hear in her account the interactions among writing, complexity, and high stakes that I suggest are at the heart of emerging mass authorship. She said:

> The clients are complex. A lot of them are homeless, jobless,
> returning from Iraq, and so they are complicated. Anything I write
> can end up as a court document and what I write can influence a
> jail sentence. So you have to kind of wrestle with the criminal justice
> system. When I'm writing I can struggle over one stupid word for half

an hour and the next day I'll come back and change it. For a half an hour you think about a word.

Here is a description from a police officer who works a downtown night beat:

> I write my reports as if I were writing a movie. I want you to be able to read my report and visualize everything that happened. I want to envelope the whole human element while I'm writing about the facts. I get enjoyment in finding the right word. That's the way I interject myself into any particular story, through the words that I use, the way that I structure the sentences that I write.

Especially powerful were reports of the effects of writing-intensity, what happens when people spend anywhere from 30 percent to 90 percent of the working day in the posture of the writer. Here are remarks from an attorney who, in addition to legal briefs, also writes regular magazine articles and speeches designed to educate the public on topics in employment law: "When I haven't written anything for several months, I say, what's wrong with me? I'm not a creative person but when I haven't written something I think I lost my ability to see relevant things."

The depth of satisfaction among many of the people I talked with was as intense as the writing act itself. Here are remarks by a freelancer about her wide-ranging fifteen-year career, which shows how writing can rival reading even in terms of vicarious experience:

> When I work with people it is really gratifying because you can open yourself up to somebody else, some other organization, some other story and absorb all of this new information, synthesize it in your head, even in your body sometimes. It feels wonderful. I feel like I've grown intellectually and even emotionally through the process. If I'm writing about anything that has any value to me personally especially, it can be gratifying to sink your teeth into a set of ideas, make them your own, and then say them in your own words. It's like learning to talk.

Everyone I interviewed could articulate specific effects that regular writing has had on their cognition. Here is a brief sample:

It crystallizes you. It crystallizes your thought.

My views have changed over time because I have had to deal with it through the writing. You have to think about it, rethink about it, and rethink about it.

I am more careful about how I say things and recognize that issues tend to be a lot more complicated.

It makes me more cautious about the words I use.

It makes me less patient with poor writing.

I tend to be more precise in my use of language in more common situations.

If the claim is to be made about literary reading that it promotes perspective taking, reflection, consciousness of language as language and develops the creativity and sensibilities of the individual, then it must be pointed out that those effects are not confined to literature and certainly not confined to reading. At work stations everywhere, people are plotting narratives, bringing characters to life, dreaming up words, throwing their voices, working, with irony and tragedy and going through mental dramas as they write.

But for now, these experiences go largely unacknowledged in the institutions in which they frequently occur. Yet conditions of mass writing and especially writing-intensity stand to shift relationships between writing and reading in the future of literacy. In and out of the workplace, reading is now more regularly embedded in acts of writing. People read in order to generate writing; we read from the posture of the writer; we write to other people who write. This is an entirely different model of literate experience and literacy from those of the past.

At least until now school-based writing has functioned largely within the ideological arrangements of a reading literacy; its moral and civic and even economic standing has been garnered indirectly through the high cultural values accorded to reading. But now the equation reverses as the value of reading comes to depend on the transactional status of writing and as literate experience throughout the life span develops increasingly in contexts of commerce, production, competition, private subsidy and surveillance. Can mass writing claim a moral authority powerful enough to transform the social institutions that were organized to serve readers over writers? The United States was founded as a nation of readers. How equipped are we now for sustaining a nation of writers?

Notes

1. See: http://www.przoom.com/news/14566/. Last accessed on 6/18/2008.
2. See Valentine (2006) and Howard (2000) for two recent, lively explorations of attitudes toward plagiarism.
3. See, for instance, Fitzgerald and Shanahan (2000); Nelson and Calfee (1998); Tierney and Shanahan (1991).

References

Angel, D., and Tannebaum, S. L. "Works Made for Hire Under S. 22." *New York Law School Law Review,* 1976–1977, 209, 209–239.

Amory, H., and Hall, D. D. (eds.). *A History of the Book in America. Volume 1: The Colonial Book in the Atlantic World.* Chapel Hill: University of North Carolina Press, 2007.

Baker, C. E. *Human Liberty and Freedom of Speech.* New York: Oxford University Press, 1989.

Brown, R. D. *The Strength of a People: The Idea of an Informed Citizenry in America 1650–1870.* Chapel Hill: University of North Carolina Press, 1996.

Bunker, M. D. *Critiquing Free Speech: First Amendment Theory and the Challenge of Interdisciplinarity.* Mahweh: Erlbaum, 2001.

Burk, D. L. "Intellectual Property and the Firm." *University of Chicago Law Review,* 2004, 71, 3–21.

Burton-Jones, A. *Knowledge Capitalism: Business, Work and Learning in the New Economy.* New York: Oxford University Press, 1999.

Cornelius, J. D. *"When I Can Read My Title Clear": Literacy, Slavery and Religion in the Antebellum South.* Columbia: University of South Carolina Press, 1991.

Finkelstein, D. "History of the Book, Authorship, Book Design and Publishing." In C. Bazerman (ed.), *Handbook on Research on Writing.* New York: Erlbaum, 2008.

Fitzgerald, J., and Shanahan, T. "Reading and Writing Relations and Their Development." *Educational Psychologist,* 2000, *35*(1), 39–50.

Furet, F., and Ozouf, J. *Reading and Writing: Literacy in France from Calvin to Jules Ferry.* New York: Cambridge University Press, 1983.

Gilmore, W. J. *Reading Becomes a Necessity of Life.* Knoxville: University of Tennessee Press, 1989.

Graff, H. J. *Labyrinths of Literacy: Reflections on Literacy Past and Present.* Pittsburgh: University of Pittsburgh Press, 1995.

Graff, H. J. *The Literacy Myth.* New York: Academic Press, 1979.

Himmelberg, R. F. (ed.). *Growth of the Regulatory State.* New York: Garland, 1994.

Howard, R. "Sexuality and Textuality: The Cultural Work of Plagiarism." *College English,* 2000, *62*(4), 473–491.

Kaestle, C. F. *Pillars of the Republic: Common Schools and American Society 1780–1860.* New York: Hill and Wang, 1983.

Long, P. O. *Openness, Secrecy, Authorship: Technical Arts and the Culture of Knowledge from Antiquity to the Renaissance.* Baltimore, Md.: Johns Hopkins University Press, 2001.

Longo, B. *Spurious Coin: A History of Science, Management, and Technical Writing.* Albany: State University of New York Press, 2000.

Monaghan, E. J. *Learning to Read and Write in Colonial America.* Amherst: University of Massachusetts Press, 2005.

National Endowment for the Arts. *Reading at Risk: A Survey of Literary Reading in America.* Research Division Report #46. Washington, D.C.: National Endowment for the Arts, 2004.

Nelson, N., and Calfee, R. C. *The Reading-Writing Connection: Ninety-Seventh Yearbook of The National Society for the Study of Education.* Chicago: University of Chicago Press, 1998.

Prahalad, C. K., and Hamel, G. "The Core Competence of the Corporation." In H. M. Zack (ed.), *Knowledge and Strategy.* Boston: Butterworth-Heinemann, 1999, pp. 41–59.

Smart, G. "Writing and the Social Formation of Economy." In C. Bazerman (ed.), *Handbook of Research on Writing.* New York: Erlbaum, 2008.

Soltow, L., and Stevens, E. *The Rise of Literacy and the Common School in the United States: A Socioeconomic Analysis to 1870.* Chicago: University of Chicago Press, 1981.

Stevens, E. W., Jr. *Grammar of the Machine: Technical Literacy and Early Industrial Expansion.* New Haven: Yale University Press, 1995.

Stewart, T. L. *Intellectual Capital: The New Wealth of Organizations.* New York: Doubleday Business, 1997.

Sunstein, C. R. *Democracy and the Problem of Free Speech.* New York: Free Press. 1993.

Tierney, R. J., and Shanahan, T. "Research on Reading-Writing Relationships: Interactions Transactions and Outcomes." In P. D. Pearson, R. Barr, M. Kamil, and P. Mosenthal (eds.), *Handbook of Reading Research, Volume Two.* New York: Longman, 1991, pp. 246–280.

Townsend, A. M., and Bennett, J. T. "Privacy, Technology and Conflict: Emerging Issues and Action in Workplace Privacy." *Journal of Labor Relations,* 2003, *24*(2), 195–208.

Valentine, K. "Plagiarism as Literacy Practice: Recognizing and Rethinking Ethical Binaries." *College Composition and Communication,* 2006, *58*(1), 89–109.

Williams, H. A. *Self Taught: African American Education in Slavery and Freedom.* Chapel Hill: University of North Carolina Press, 2005.

7

How Writing Is Remaking Reading

IN 1982, HENRY LEONARD[1] WAS HIRED INTO THE SPECIAL COLLECTIONS DEPARTMENT OF A HISTORICAL LIBRARY. He spent his days preparing exhibit notes and composing letters to researchers inquiring about the rare books under his care. By 2005, he was director of Web services for the same library. These days, he writes eight-hundred-word essays and fictionalized blogs that serve as conceptual portals to digitized materials. "The idea," he said, "is to get what we have into people's living rooms." Leonard writes more often, in more genres, and toward more venues than he did twenty-five years ago. But more profoundly, through his work, he is changing an institution that was designed to think like readers into one that thinks like a writer. "Instead of collections," he observed, "now we think about audiences."

Like Leonard, more and more Americans are spending more and more of their time in the posture of the writer. As the nature of work in the United States has changed—toward making and managing information and knowledge usually in globalized settings—intense pressure has come to bear on the productive side of literacy, the writing side (Brandt, 2004; Drucker, 2003). For perhaps the first time in the history of mass literacy, writing seems to be eclipsing reading as the literate experience of consequence. What happens when writing (and not just reading) becomes the grounds of mass literate experience, when more and more people "think about audiences" as part of their daily, routine engagement with literacy? How does a societal shift in time and energy toward writing affect the ways that people develop their literacy and understand its worth? And finally, how does the ascendancy of a writing-based literacy create tensions in a society whose institutions were organized around a reading literacy, around a presumption that readers would be many and writers would be few?

As teachers of language and literacy, we tend to think of reading and writing as mutually supportive processes. They both draw on similar underlying cognitive and linguistic skills and both rely on similar social, pragmatic, and rhetorical resources (Fitzgerald and Shanahan, 2000; Nelson and Calfee, 1998; Tierney and Shanahan, 1991). Reading almost always shows up in the company of writing in school, intensively so in academic assignments at the college level. And it is not unusual to be asked in school to demonstrate reading comprehension by writing answers to test questions. Obviously there can be no reading without writing and no writing without reading. And despite the shaky research, there remains widespread belief that to write well one must read well—that writers learn to write largely through reading.

So because as a group we have been particularly invested in the similarities between reading and writing, we have spent less time thinking about how reading and writing can be in competition with each other, how they can be antagonistic to one another, how the uses and practices that grow up around the one might challenge and change the other. But from certain angles and increasingly within the lived experience of ordinary literates, this is what is happening. The heritage of reading is being undermined by the heritage of writing. While the NEA (*Reading at Risk,* 2004) and others would simply say, in alarm, that less reading is being done, based on their recent surveys, I would suggest instead that reading is being undone by writing—at least as reading has been traditionally understood.

As a demonstration, let's continue with the literacy account of librarian Henry Leonard. Leonard was born in 1950 into the high age of mass reading. He was raised by working-class parents eager for him to be a good student. Leonard said he "vowed by the age of six I would read every book in the town library" and "I got a lot of praise for reading books from my mother and the library staff." As a young adult, he worked as a custodian of books, first as a bookseller after college and eventually as a library archivist. Over the last dozen years, however, he has been increasingly turning to writing to manage his work—as public funding for his library has tightened and computers have altered the ways people seek information. Leonard uses writing not merely to mediate relationships between collections and distant readers, but to generate and condition the readership itself. He uses writing to drum up business and gather support. "I write all day," he explained, "and a lot of the writing I do brings in money" in the form of grants, press releases, a blog (which he calls "an information delivery mechanism"), and family-history materials that the library sells to amateur genealogists. These days it is writing that garners praise from the library staff as they turn their attention to newfangled rhetorical problems, such as figuring out the right textual formats to use to ensure that the Google search engine would detect their collections. As Leonard relies on writing to sustain reading on an institutional level, the effects spill into his own literacy practices. He spends weekends and evenings at home answering e-mail traffic on the library's Web site or messaging with staff ("The conversation is always on," he observed), and he increasingly finds it "kind of a chore to read a book," preferring spontaneous downloads from Gutenberg.org.

We can see in this account a classic clash in the auspices under which mass reading and mass writing have historically been undertaken. At the risk of oversimplifying, reading has been for being good—being good in worship, in citizenship, in school, in work—being good as in being well socialized, well informed, well behaved, well cultured, well parented, well positioned, well protected, well deserving, well trusted, well educated (Graff, 1979; Soltow and Stevens, 1981). In fact, any kind of well-being one can think of has been associated at one time or other with reading. We see this legacy in the relationship of Leonard to his mother and the librarians, figures with the traditional responsibility of nurturing the young by teaching the value of reading and its connection to being good (Cobb, 2000; Kerber, 1976; Passet, 1994; Robbins, 2004; Williams, 2005). These values reach back into the earliest sponsoring institutions of a reading literacy, notably the church and the common school. This tradition was heavily associated with Protestant settlements in New England and was still well intact when Leonard was growing up in New England in the '50s and '60s. Further, the institution of the free public library enshrined the value of reading and its relationship to the rights and duties of citizens to be responsibly informed participants in a democratic government. In the arrangements of a reading literacy, books have value because their goodness can rub off on readers and it is this moral value that created the economy Leonard entered after college as a purveyor of books, first as a bookseller and eventually a librarian himself. He was able to turn literacy's moral value into a living.

But mass writing does not share in this moral legacy of mass reading. Mass writing has always been for work, for production, for output, earning, profit, publicity, practicality, record keeping, buying, and selling; and increasingly writing itself is the product that is bought and sold as it embodies knowledge, information, invention, service, social relations, news—that is, the products of the new economy (Brandt, 2007; Furet and Ouzouf, 1983; Yates, 2005). Writing is less for good than it is a good. Reading might make you more productive, but writing *is* more productive. It is for itself and its value is for itself. In fact, it is the commercial or transactional value of writing, its materiality, its fungibility, its amenability to work, wage, and market, that make writing unique among the so-called language arts and give it such a different cultural history from reading, one with great tangible effects on literacy now. As Leonard's library became increasingly entrepreneurial, in the face of significant reductions in public funding, and as the library had to compete with other cultural institutions, also poorly funded, for the loyalty of clients, as its public viability became linked to its public visibility, writing in the library intensified. What Leonard knew about reading and readers had to be converted more elaborately and functionally into something that could be proactively transacted, into something that could generate resources, that is, into writing.

We can also see traces in Leonard's account of how writing almost always depends on powerful patrons with whom writers enter into some sort of give and take relationship (Long, 2001). Here I am especially interested in the commercial enterprise Google, which essentially serves as the publisher and distributor of much of Leonard's writing and the library holdings in general. In the new conditions, the library can not merely hold its holdings; like a writer, it must publish them. And that projects the library into the realm of commercial patronage. Historically, writing has always taken place in that realm, within client-patron relationships, whether with scribes who copied holy manuscripts for the glory of the church (Clanchy, 1993); or early authors who would dedicate their work to the wealthy benefactors who provided their livelihood (Long, 2001); or, ghostwriters who sell away their authorship rights (Brandt, 2007); or modern authors who split copyrights and profits with publishers (Rose, 1994; Saunders, 1992); or modern-day, just-for-the-fun-of-it bloggers who post their texts on commercially sponsored Web sites (Rainie, n.d.). Writers always need benefactors and underwriters, and benefactors and underwriters always need writers. As the library increasingly saw its readers more as clients or customers, its interests dovetailed with Google. Google was there to broadcast the library's wares in the marketplace of ideas and information and to expand its own reach and value in the gesture. In exchange, the librarians had to package their wares to certain technical specifications—they had to learn how to make their texts Google-friendly.

Finally, in this account, I wish to point out how, over the course of Leonard's career, his own reading gets increasingly repositioned within writing. Reading doesn't go away. It is repositioned. We can see this repositioning throughout his account, but most dramatically, it seems to me, in the reference to Gutenberg.org. These days, Leonard prefers to do his traditional elective reading not through books but on his writing machines, including, he mentioned to me, handheld devices that he carries with him. This is one literal way that many of us read now, from the position of the writer, with our hands on keypads and through the same material mediums through which we write. The two activities now take place in the same posture, almost indistinguishable from one another. Concurrently, Leonard writes now more intensively in response to other people's writing ("the conversation is always on"), which is another way that reading is repositioned within acts of writing, readers repositioned within writers. The visit to the digitized library is initiated by writing. Library users are encouraged to be writers through the many interactive features of the library Web site. These days, the reading experience seems not to be complete somehow without the writing (Benkler, 2006; Lessig, 2004). The fact that so many of us are now writing to each other as part of daily, mass-literate experience is one of the most profound characteristics of the new mass literacy and one that most starkly differentiates mass writing from mass reading.

So what I am suggesting is that writing literacy takes a different course from reading literacy because of the ways that it has been sponsored and valued and that as it rises in prominence, we need to consider how it might alter the ways literacy develops over the life span, how it will reposition reading within writing, how these shifts will change the ways that literacy finds meaning and value in our institutions and social life, and how in turn that might change our institutions and social life. It is more than a little interesting to me and more than a mere coincidence from my perspective that Henry Leonard's young adult son operates his own Web site on which he writes extensively about rare animals and where he answers readers' questions and occasionally sells from the Web site; that he delayed entrance to college so that he could travel to upgrade his knowledge in support of this enterprise; and that in his early twenties he authored a book published and distributed by a private corporation. So we must remark on the differences between the literacy patterns of the father as a youth and his son, the sponsors of their literacy, as well as the operative values in which their significant literacy learning and practices occur, a difference that I would call writing over reading.

In the rest of this chapter I want to continue to explore the implications of this transition in the history of mass literacy. As I mentioned earlier, reading in the United States historically has been regarded as a universal right and responsibility, largely because of its association with the universalizing campaign of church (particularly, in this society evangelical Protestantism) and the universalizing campaign of the state, in the form of compulsory schooling (Soltow and Stevens, 1981). Reading has been regarded as critical to one's ability to worship freely and fully, to pursue knowledge, and to fulfill the duties of citizenship. No such universalizing ideologies have sanctioned writing, and writing has been much less of a concern of church or state (Monaghan, 2005). State investment in citizen reading over time has been staggeringly greater than its investment in citizen writing. In addition, legal protections of mass reading are much more entrenched in case law than protections of mass writing. Writing rights are actually secondhand: they are derived mostly from the rights of citizen readers to pursue information and knowledge without government constraint. Writing is valued and protected for what it can do for readers, much less so in terms of what it can do for writers (Sunstein, 1993).

Major subsidies for mass writing have come not mainly from church and state but from employers, public and especially private: first in the trading and commercial economies of the new republic, then escalating with industrialism, the growth of bureaucracies, the centrality of written communication in managing and coordinating large systems, and intensifying especially over the last fifty years as knowledge work has taken over the U.S. economy, making writing a chief means and a chief output of production (Beniger, 1986; Yates, 1989). Services are bought and sold through texts. Consumers are cultivated and educated through texts. Texts accompany physical products in the forms of warranties and instructions. Beyond work, writing on the Internet, including elective, citizen writing, is being commodified, subsidized by news organizations and other commercial sponsors who organize behind the scenes monitors to instigate and moderate the writing even as they find ways to advertise merchandise to people who are in the act of writing (Barlow, 2007; Solove, 2004; Wallace, 2004). Historically, this interlacing of writing literacy with commercial enterprise and wealth production means that workplaces and other commercial locations may well be the place where the most teaching and learning of writing and certainly the most subsidy for writing has always occurred across time and under conditions and reigning values much different from those associated with the sponsors of reading literacy. For certain, the transition of this society to computer-based writing and Internet communication could not have happened as quickly as it has without the aggressive role of workplaces in teaching these new skills to a general population.

It would be hard to underestimate the intense level of teaching and learning going on right now around writing in the workplace, where so much of an organization's reputation and value rides on written texts and where investment focuses so heavily on so-called human capital, including, especially, intellectual and communicative skill. Over the past couple of years I have talked to forty-five workaday people, virtually all of whom situate significant aspects of their literacy experience and development in relationship to writing at work. Teaching and learning about writing at work comes in many forms:

in formal classes; in homegrown style guides; in visits from product reps; in professional seminars; in e-mail exchanges or desk-side visits with IT staff; in consultation with content experts; in the editing marks of a supervisor; in a conversation with a peer or coauthor; in meetings with funding agencies; in a demonstration by a secretary, in what one person called "distributive education," in which somebody who just learned something new brings it back to the group; by trial and error; by observation and osmosis; through inventional heuristics; via text models and role models; by getting feedback from clients or other audiences; by having to justify one's composing decisions; or by reflecting privately on what went right or wrong. Teaching writing and supporting writing is often an explicit responsibility of supervisors, whose instructional styles range from explicit directions or corrections to more gentle strategies, such as those of one manager, now retired, who recalled giving some of his employees copies of *Reader's Digest* to encourage vocabulary building or to recommend emulation of particular styles.

Learning writing is necessitated on the job by a range of pressures, including general reorganization, changes in responsibility, layoffs, desire to move up or move on, adoption of new technologies or procedures, the emergence of new genres, expanding or diversifying audiences or constituencies, changes in regulatory climates, heightened competition with other firms or agents, labor activism, and what one person called just plain old "hard experience." (So the learning environment for writing is quite dynamic, even turbulent, for many people in the workplace.) Learning was especially necessitated by the major role that writing itself plays in teaching and informing others, so there was much reading and study and research pertaining to subject matter, particularly among technical writers, analysts, attorneys, trainers, sales and marketing people, and freelance writers. In workplaces, writing is sometimes tested as part of a job application or promotion review. The process of writing is discussed vigorously. Acts of writing take place in plain view in many cases. Potential teachers outnumber students most of the time. Texts are evaluated all the time, informally and formally, and at every stage of production, sometimes by many people, who, in some settings, literally stamp their approval in the margins of a text as it works its way around the organizational chart. Writing talent gets noticed, recruited, even at times rewarded. Things learned about writing and through writing at work travel outward into networks of families and friends and vice versa. I interviewed one person who called his son away from high school for help when preparation of an important presentation hit a technical glitch. So these are intense teaching and learning environments where there is a lot at stake. Further, writing done at work comes to shape people's language habits in general, as well as the ways they might think about civic issues, and even the ways they see themselves. Here are just a few responses to my simple question: What effect does your work writing have on you?

> It crystallizes you. It crystallizes your thought.
>
> My views have changed over time because I have had to deal with it through the writing. You have to think about it, rethink about it, and rethink about it.
>
> I am more careful about how I say things and recognize that issues tend to be a lot more complicated.
>
> It makes me more cautious about the words I use.
>
> I tend to be more precise in my use of language in more common situations.
>
> When I haven't written anything for several months, I say, what's wrong with me? I'm not a creative person but when I haven't written something I think I [have] lost my ability to see relevant things.

Above all it is in the everyday workplace where the power of authorship—in all of its rhetorical, aesthetic, and ethical complexity—is experienced now, quietly, often invisibly, but very often profoundly on a mass scale. It is the way that contemporary workplaces are organized for writing; the needs of organizations to achieve big goals and solve big problems through writing; the placement of powerful technologies under the hands of individuals; and the position of workaday writers themselves as hardworking mental mediators of these big forces that makes workplaces such potent sites for the development of literacy and authorship. That these experiences are happening to so many people at the same time is what makes mass writing and the ways it is being produced so potentially consequential culturally, socially, and politically.

I have gone on at length about the range and depth of literacy learning at work—its connection to the human development of millions of Americans right now—to underscore that workplaces are indeed schools for literacy where much potential is at stake. But they are not schools with the same universalizing mandates as those that developed around the public school and its project of a mass reading literacy. In the workplace, literacy instruction is organized around production, so the opportunities you have to learn, the levels of subsidy and support that are provided, usually depend on your location and your value in the production process with the most learning and the most support usually happening at the top and the least learning and the least support usually happening at the bottom. While some may point out, and with good reason, that the same thing goes on in public education, in the workplace this stratification will find no ideological counterweight, no political pushback. Because literacy in the workplace is mostly valued through the heritage of its production side, its writing side, it is treated as a form of labor and a raw material in the manufacturing of transactional products. And if human literacy is developed and subsidized unequally as a byproduct of this arrangement, it is rarely treated as a cause for societal alarm, let alone lawsuits. So, for instance, in the educational corporation where I work, if you are a professor who has remained fairly computer illiterate for, say, the full twenty-five years you have taught there, you can get help at any hour of the day or night, free of charge, rendered patiently, even deferentially, by stacks of technical support staff who will answer the phone or an e-mail or even make a house call to teach you how to write with an array of hardware and software that is also supplied to you by the university at your desk or even at home or at the many free and open kiosks erected throughout campus. But if you are, say, a new immigrant working as a custodian and you are lucky enough to get into one of the few, oversubscribed ESL courses now being offered to employees, your access to instruction could be cut off if you haven't learned English in sixteen months. Also, the use of campus computers by custodians during work hours is forbidden in the work rules and can result in termination. But who bats an eye about this? When seen from the perspective of work, literacy development becomes a particularly fragile resource connected to economic class and economic vicissitude. These inequities are not confined to differences between professors and custodians. Several people I interviewed talked pointedly of the ebbing and flowing of their writing literacy as they, for example, lost jobs at big corporations and became self-employed entrepreneurs or shifted from rather affluent private businesses into public sector work or moved from student status at a university with its wealth of cutting-edge resources into the bare-bones offices of nonprofit agencies. Opportunity to write, incentive to write, access to materials, access to audiences, access to learning all could wax and wane significantly. Today the tightening association between socioeconomic status and literacy, the growing gaps in wealth between the literacy-haves and the literacy have-nots, stems in part from the patterns of access and investment that accompany the role of writing in economic production.

If the heritage of writing literacy favors stratification of access and subsidy, it also favors control and surveillance in ways that again can affect reading, but much more controversially when it does. Because employers buy the time of workplace writers and own the equipment on which they write, the words that people produce at work don't really belong to them, even though, if the research I am doing is any guide, it certainly feels to them that they do (Angel and Tannenbaum, 1976–77). Many people talked to me about their sense of responsibility as well as their intense pleasure and pride, in some cases their sense of civic agency that comes through work writing. As I suggested earlier, they achieve authorship even as they write in obscurity, mostly, in fact, in anonymity and often under the name of higher-ups who will be credited with the writing. As academics, we might be most familiar with provisions of copyright law that give professional writers control over their intellectual creations. But most workaday writers labor under different provisions of that law, under the work made for hire provisions, by which authorship or ownership rights over written products (and the ideas contained in them) accrue to the material provider, typically the employer (Burk, 2004; Wishner, 1995).

That is one reason that there is such a weak tradition of privacy rights in the workplace, especially when it comes to writing. Surveillance of employees' personal e-mailing and Web browsing at work, which has been much in the news of late, is justified in large measure by the fact that workers are using equipment owned by employers, which gives the employers the right to surveillance and the right to punish unauthorized writing. First Amendment rights in the workplace are likewise weak, and again in part because of the tradition of viewing writing there not as expression, but as forms of labor and product (Wallace, 2004). The Supreme Court has ruled the First Amendment largely inoperable in the workplace, even in government workplaces, because, according to the judges, we do not really think or write or speak at work as citizens or free beings but rather as willingly coerced corporate voices. At least in our official capacities, we don't write as ourselves at work. We don't necessarily mean what we say. According to the courts, you can't protect something that doesn't

exist, and free expression at work, except interestingly in labor relations, pretty much doesn't exist (Baker, 1989).

To sum up, especially over the last fifty years, we have been part
of a literacy campaign that is turning us into a nation of mass writers. This campaign is occurring under the auspices of institutions that
operate according to different rationales, mandates, and legal traditions from the ones that grew up around mass reading—including, of
course, school traditions. Especially because writing literacy depends
so much on sponsors who retain ownership and say-so over the materials of its production, mass writing enjoys far less independence and
far less government protection than reading, even as the opportunities for authorship are coming to common people for the first time.
As writing literacy continues its ascendancy in economic and social
power, reading will continue to be folded into writing, perhaps los-
ing its independence and government protection in the process as it is
brought in line with a different ideological heritage. At the very least,
the course of individual literacy development is undergoing radical
change, not as some suggest because of new technologies but along
with them. Increasingly we will learn to write by writing and by writing to other people who also write. Increasingly we will read in order to
write. Increasingly our literacy will develop in contexts of competition
brought on by mass authorship. These arrangements can be exciting,
even, from certain angles, democratizing. Certainly librarian Henry
Leonard sees things that way. He is sharing knowledge now with many
more people and many different kinds of people than he did in 1982
and that pleases him, along with the excitement of rethinking and
retooling the library as a social institution—a process that has stimulated him intellectually and greatly amplified his own literacy along
the way. But as our literacy increasingly falls to entrepreneurialism,
private sponsors, workplaces, Web administrators, and the advertisers they depend on, those sponsors will become the stewards of a new
mass literacy. How this transition plays out and how governments,

schools, and other institutions adjust is yet to be seen. At the very least these stewards need to recognize the role they are playing and what is at stake. They need to partner with schools in protecting and equalizing access to literacy, which remains—in both its writing form and its reading form—an astonishing human resource central to our democratic possibilities.

Note

1. This is a pseudonym. Henry Leonard was interviewed in June 2005 as part of a larger interview project that asks workaday Americans to reflect on the writing they do on and off the job.

References

Angel, D., and Tannenbaum, S. L. "Works Made for Hire under S. 22." *New York Law School Law Review,* 1976–77, *209,* 209–239.

Baker, C. E. *Human Liberty and Freedom of Speech.* New York: Oxford University Press, 1989.

Barlow, A. *The Rise of the Blogosphere.* Westport, Conn.: Prager, 2007.

Beniger, J. F. *The Control Revolution: Technological and Economic Origins of the Information Society.* Cambridge, Mass.: Harvard University Press, 1986.

Benkler, Y. *The Wealth of Networks: How Social Production Transforms Markets and Freedom.* New Haven, Conn.: Yale University Press, 2006.

Brandt, D. "Drafting U.S. Literacy." *College English,* 2004, *66,* 485–502.

Brandt, D. "Who's the President? Ghostwriting and Shifting Values in Literacy." *College English,* 2007, *69,* 549–571.

Burk, D. L. "Intellectual Property and the Firm." *University of Chicago Law Review,* 2004, *71,* 3–21.

Clanchy, M. T. *From Memory to Written Record.* New York: Wiley-Blackwell, 1993.

Cobb, A. *Listening to Our Grandmothers' Stories.* Lincoln: University of Nebraska Press, 2000.

Drucker, P. F. "The Knowledge Society." In Peter F. Drucker, *A Functioning Society: Selections from Sixty-five Years of Writing on Community, Society, and Polity.* New Brunswick, N.J.: Transaction, 2003, pp. 147–194.

Fitzgerald, J., and Shanahan, T. "Reading and Writing Relations and Their Development." *Educational Psychologist,* 2000, *35*(1), 39–50.

Furet, F., and Ozouf, J. *Reading and Writing: Literacy in France from Calvin to Jules Ferry.* New York: Cambridge University Press, 1983.

Graff, H. J. *The Literacy Myth: Literacy and Social Structure in the Nineteenth-Century City.* New York: Academic Press, 1979.

Kerber, L. "The Republican Mother." *American Quarterly*, 1976, *28*, 187–205.

Lessig, L. *Free Culture: The Nature and Future of Creativity.* New York: Penguin, 2004.

Long, P. O. *Openness, Secrecy, Authorship: Technical Arts and the Culture of Knowledge from Antiquity to the Renaissance.* Baltimore, Md.: Johns Hopkins University Press, 2001.

Monaghan, E. J. *Learning to Read and Write in Colonial America.* Amherst: University of Massachusetts Press, 2005.

National Endowment for the Arts. *Reading at Risk: A Survey of Literary Reading in America.* National Endowment for the Arts Research Division Report #46. Washington, D.C.: National Endowment for the Arts, 2004.

Nelson, N., and Calfee, R. C. (eds.) *The Reading-Writing Connection.* Chicago: University of Chicago Press, 1998.

Passet, J. *Cultural Crusaders: Women Librarians in the American West 1900–1917.* Albuquerque: University of New Mexico Press, 1994.

Rainie, L. "The State of Blogging." Pew Center for the Study of the Internet and American Life. Available at www.pewinternet.org. Last accessed on 7/16/2007.

Robbins, S. *Managing Literacy, Mothering America.* Pittsburgh, Pa.: University of Pittsburgh Press, 2004.

Rose, M. "The Author as Proprietor." In B. Sherman and A. Strowel (eds.), *Of Authors and Origins.* Oxford: Clarendon Press, 1994, pp. 23–55.

Saunders, D. *Authorship and Copyright.* New York: Routledge, 1992.

Solove, D. J. *The Digital Person: Technology and Privacy in the Information Age.* New York: New York University Press, 2004.

Sunstein, C. R. *Democracy and the Problem of Free Speech.* New York: Free Press, 1993.

Soltow, L., and Stevens, E. *The Rise of Literacy and the Common School in the United States: A Socioeconomic Analysis to 1870.* Chicago: University of Chicago Press, 1981.

Tierney, R. J., and Shanahan, T. "Research on the Reading-Writing Relationship: Interactions, Transactions, and Outcomes." In P. David Pearson, Rebecca Barr, Michael L. Kamil, and Peter B. Mosenthal (eds.), *Handbook of Reading Research, Volume II.* New York: Longman, 1991, pp. 245–280.

Wallace, P. *The Internet in the Workplace: How New Technology Is Transforming Work.* New York: Cambridge University Press, 2004.

Williams, H. A. *Self-Taught: African American Education in Slavery and Freedom.* Chapel Hill: University of North Carolina Press, 2005.

Wishner, C. L. "Whose Work Is It Anyway? Revisiting Community for Creative Non-Violence *v.* Reid in Defining the Employer-Employee Relationship Under the 'Work Made for Hire' Doctrine." *Hofstra Labor Law Journal*, 1995, *12*, 393–420.

Yates, J. *Control Through Communication: The Rise of System in American Management.* Baltimore, Md.: Johns Hopkins University Press, 1989.

Yates, J. *Structuring the Information Age.* Baltimore, Md.: Johns Hopkins University Press, 2005.

CONCLUSION: AN EXCERPT FROM
LITERACY IN AMERICAN LIVES

FOR MUCH OF ITS CAREER, LITERACY IN THE UNITED STATES found its value principally in social and political contexts rather than economic ones. Not an end in itself, literacy was a useful mechanism for religious initiation and nation building, a means to assimilate people into dominant modes of conduct and beliefs. The emblematic value of literacy was at least as important as its practical value, as its presence was a signal that a certain kind of socialization—a certain kind of capitulation—had occurred. As Graff (1979) and others have shown, literacy did begin to be incorporated more aggressively into the needs of an industrializing economy toward the end of the nineteenth century. However, its value at that time continued to reside mostly in its socializing power, including its capacity to assist in the assimilation of immigrants and to sort people in such a way that access and reward for literacy continued to favor the entrenched. Throughout this economic transition, literacy retained its connection to tradition and to social conformity and stability. As it linked citizens to an official cultural past, traditional knowledge, and centralized authority, literacy served as a counterbalance to the social disruptions and instabilities that industrialism was introducing. Although reading and writing were emerging as forms of skilled labor, literacy remained peripheral to most work. In short, for most of the history of mass literacy, its value remained only indirectly instrumental—going through the rigors of becoming literate mattered more than being able to trade on it (in fact, the more literate you were, the less you were likely to have to trade on it). Like the economic sphere in premarket economies (Polanyi, 1944), literacy was deeply embedded in the forms and functions of cultural cohesion. Its practices, meanings, materials, and effects derived mainly from its conservative and conserving role.

However, as the rise of the market economy rearranged relationships among economic, social, and political spheres, it brought radical pressures to bear on literacy. Literacy became directly and deeply implicated in economic life for many mutually reinforcing reasons. Buying and selling involved many more people in recording, moving, and promoting information. Readers became targets, both as audiences for advertising and as purchasers of literacy-based commodities. Although always an aspect of literacy in American society, its economic meanings surged prominently as the twentieth century unfolded. At the same time, a market mentality was helping to separate out forms of human resources, including literacy skills, as commodities in themselves. Labor came to be treated as a cost in production rather than a value added during production. In increasing numbers, people found their mental and scribal skills rated and tagged for market to employers. Just as the economic sphere unmoored from the laws and logic of social control, literacy, too, gained more recognizable status as a productive force within the new system.

These developments tied literacy less to tradition and social stability and more to competition and change. Instead of serving as a counterbalance during periods of excessive or rapid economic transformation, literacy came to play an integral role in transformation; it became a major catalyst for changes in communicative and economic relations. As the original "information processors," human beings in technological societies saw the basic abilities to read and write drawn deeply into the assumptions of work. And, like other technologies vital to an information economy, forms of reading and writing were subject to rounds of obsolescence, upgrades, overhauls, augmentation, rearrangements, and replacements.

Of course, it might rightly be observed that literacy has always stimulated cultural disruption, especially in those on whom it has been imposed. And wherever and whenever new uses and technologies of writing have occurred, they have created new social circuits, affected the status of old ones, and set off other, far-reaching reverberations in intellectual and material life (see Martin,). However, in the twentieth century, the alliance of literacy with economic change intensified, the pace of change quickened, and the impact of the association broadened to affect more people than ever before. On the one hand, it would be overreaching to make literacy the cause of all the economic and social changes of the twentieth century—just as it is overreaching to make literacy the solution for all of our economic and social problems. On the other hand, it would be equally wrong to underestimate the role of literacy as an enabling mechanism for much of what happened—especially as literacy came to be capitalized as a profit-bearing resource. It especially would be wrong to underestimate the pressures that these developments have brought to bear on contemporary literacy learning. . . .

The commandeering of literacy by economic interests in the twentieth century registers most profoundly in the changing networks through which literacy has been sponsored. Sponsors are embodied in the materials of reading and writing, the institutional aegises and rationales under which learning is carried out, the histories by which practices arrive at the scenes of learning, the causes to which teachers and learners put their efforts, and the advantages, both direct and indirect, that stand to be won by the sponsors themselves. As we have seen, sponsors organize and administer stratified systems of opportunity and access. They raise the stakes for literacy in rivalries for advantage.

They certify and often decertify literacy. Sponsors can be benefactors but also extortionists—and sometimes both in the same form. . . .

By the new millennium, economic competition had taken more and more control of the access and reward system for literacy, including the standards against which everyone's literacy is measured and valued. The full implications of these developments must be made more relevant in thinking about literacy today. Here are several implications that are especially striking and far reaching:

First, literacy is being sponsored in much different ways than it was in the past. Through most of its history, literacy was affiliated with a few strong cultural agents—education, religion, local commerce. It tended to be learned in the same contexts in which it was intended to be practiced. Now, sponsors of literacy are more prolific, diffused, and heterogeneous. Commercial sponsors abound and reach all geographical locations, often through channels of television, radio, and computer—as do other big arms of literacy, the national government and international conglomerates. Whereas people used to move to literacy, literacy now moves to people. . . . A proliferation of sponsors also means that people who move—sometimes from culture to culture—transport their literacy from one context to another or must adapt and amalgamate practices learned in one sphere to meet the new demands of another sphere. Global communications and increased migrations can only intensify this process in the future. Schools are no longer the major disseminators of literacy. Literacy instruction needs to develop from a sense of a new role for schools, as a place where the ideological complexities (including the inequities) of literacy sponsorship are sorted through and negotiated. Basic literate ability requires the ability to position and reposition oneself among literacy's sponsoring agents as well as among competing forms of communication.

Second, the diversification of work, especially parental work, brings various kinds of materials, instruments, and other resources into homes where they can be appropriated into teaching and learning.

Current adult and family literacy campaigns emphasize the connection between children's school success and parental literacy and encourage parents to spend more time reading to their young children. In some communities, new mothers receive complimentary children's books when they are discharged from the maternity ward. And much effort is expended in early childhood education programs to engage low-income and undereducated mothers in child-centered literacy practices. These campaigns broadcast images of parents, usually mothers, relaxing in chairs or perching at bedsides, reading storybooks to young children. Although *Literacy in American Lives* has turned up plenty of evidence of recreational reading by parents with children, home literacy overall also was strongly associated in memory with parental work. When children saw adults in their households reading and writing, it was often work related. It also was through adult work or work-related education that literacy materials, extensive or spare, entered households. Though not always the focus of explicit instruction and not often school oriented, work-related reading and writing provided children real-world information about how literacy functions. More important, these encounters often brought at least some children into contact with the material assets and social power of major literacy sponsors—corporations, industries, merchants, governments, and universities. . . . .

The relationship between parental work and literacy must play a more prominent role in approaches to family literacy. For one thing, this relationship can illuminate the role of men in literacy learning, a dimension that is often overlooked when family literacy is linked solely to the nurture of preschool children. The historically privileged position that men have enjoyed in education and employment made fathers in many households the conduits of specialized skills and materials that could be of interest and use to other family members. This especially became true as more and more men worked in information and knowledge production. Women who worked in subordinate positions, typing, filing, and dispatching documents and other forms of print, could borrow skills and concepts from more highly educated men for whom they worked, turning this knowledge into assets for their families. . . . As late-twentieth-century women gained more regular access to higher education and professional work, they could bring associated materials and skills directly into the context of child rearing. Now, especially, computers bring literacy resources, often work related, into private dwellings. The circulation of work-related literacy in households has contributed significantly to the diffusion of formal knowledge and literacy practices in this society. When we appreciate the connection between parental work and household literacy, we might better see why it is so urgent to make expanding education and employment opportunities (and not just bedtime story reading) a cornerstone of family literacy programs. As was suggested in an earlier chapter, the resources of workplaces could be better recruited into the literacy development of adults and their children. Beyond donating often obsolete computer equipment to community organizations, workplaces could more genuinely increase access to literacy resources and human development opportunities for all workers and their families. This seems especially important in public institutions such as schools, universities, and government and health agencies.

Third, the pattern of literacy sponsorship in a parent's lifetime may bear little resemblance to the patterns in his or her child's lifetime, and the same with teacher and student. In a society inured to change, the significance of this phenomenon should not be overlooked. Mass literacy arose from the premise that print would function, in the words of Soltow and Stevens, as "social cement" (1981, p. 193). The stable, fixed nature of print, its authority in religion and statehood, and its effectiveness for rote learning all made literacy salient in maintaining traditions and passing down official versions of experience. For many generations, reading took place principally as what Gilmore (1989) identified as an intensive practice, as most people read the same small set of texts (mostly religious) repeatedly over a lifetime. But as commercial culture grew in the late-eighteenth and nineteenth centuries, more extensive and serial reading became more prominent, a trend that intensified significantly in the United States over the twentieth century as paperbacks and magazines became big business. The more people could read and the more specific tastes could be addressed by print advertisers, the more periodicals proliferated and the more readership fragmented. The development of the children's literature industry, including special children's sections in public libraries, helped to stratify reading experiences by generation. Specialized knowledge and political and ethnic activism also broke reading publics into smaller audiences (Kaestle and others, 1991). But more than the fracturing of reading audiences, it has been revolutions in communication technologies as well as the competition for new uses of the resources of reading and writing that drive the biggest generational wedges in literacy learning. . . .

Technological change around literacy has had the fastest and most disruptive impact from a generational standpoint. As if in a kaleidoscope, reading and writing shift with each new communication option, including telephone, radio, film, television, home video, and computer. The ages at which people make contact with influential new technologies heavily influence literacy learning. Radio, when it was first introduced, brought news and narrative to millions of listeners, and, on the one hand, people I interviewed who were born in the 1920s and 1930s credited radio with stimulating their interest in reading and writing. On the other hand, many members of this same cohort dismissed television, which arrived later in their lives, as irrelevant or even deleterious to their literacy. By the 1950s and 1960s, narrative and news shifted to the new technology of television as commercial radio turned mostly to music. People raised in the 1960s and 1970s were more apt to name television and not radio as a strong and largely positive influence on their reading and writing. As the first genuinely digital youth generation comes to consciousness, early literacy experiences embedded in computer and Internet use undoubtedly will give that generation's literacy a different quality from that of members of older generations. Mass media and new communication technologies touch members of all generations, of course, but the meaning of that contact and its capacity to affect literacy learning seems strongly linked to age. This is partly because of the ways that new communication technologies jockey against or sometimes appropriate the social functions of earlier technologies, but it also has to do with what part of the individual life span is making contact with the new technology and how. Here is another arena in which competition—in this case, the competition posed to reading and writing by other communication options—affects the basic processes of literacy learning. Young people today encounter a learning climate in which reading and writing coexist with a greater number of alternative communicative systems, and this climate inevitably affects the meanings and mechanisms of literacy in young lives in distinctive ways (see Cremin, 1990). . . . Parents and teachers must prepare young people to be writers and readers in forums and genres that they themselves have not necessarily learned in. And this teaching takes place in technological and communicative contexts that are themselves fast-moving and unsteady underfoot. More people now carry around in their life experiences accumulating strata of contact with multiple writing technologies and genres. Indeed, the twentieth century is a virtual junkyard of recessive and abandoned communication materials; the twenty-first century will be the same. The difficulties inherent in literacy learning and teaching under these unprecedented conditions should not be simplified.

Fourth, the insinuation of market forces into the meanings and methods by which literacy is learned poses crucial ethical and policy questions for public education. Especially dangerous are the ways that education is now being cast as a privatized and individualized commodity—something that families obtain singly for their children. This approach to education obliterates the memory of how much opportunity for literacy and schooling have depended on generous public subsidy—how much that history rides in the backgrounds of families now enjoying the greatest private rewards in the information age. We especially must scrutinize the ways that market forces can cause racial injustices to snowball. Two generations ago, high school became widely available to the mass of white citizens. Thus began the accumulation of education that powered the economic transformations that in turn created more opportunities for education for those poised to seize them. Advanced literacy and education, especially for men, began to pay off in many segments of white society. Yet two generations ago, African Americans and other people of color were, by law and custom, typically excluded from the opportunities of high school education or routed into vocational and industrial training. Literacy and education continued to spread anyway among African Americans, especially in the middle class, but because of segregation could not pay off in the expected ways. A lot of things were changing in the American economy of the early-twentieth century but not its outlook on race. Government at all levels underinvested in the education of nonwhite citizens and used schools to enforce low expectations. People of color, black, brown, and red, were expected to stay in their place: mostly landless and performing lower-skilled, lower-wage manual and domestic service. This treatment pertained in both private and public enterprises, including the military, through the first half of the twentieth century. People of color who attained advanced education were expected to keep it among their own; their literacy, as a national resource, was appropriated and exploited only in extreme emergencies (like war) and was not systematically amplified or rewarded by the mainstream economy. The capacity to parlay the resources of literacy into economic assets and intergenerational security was seriously curtailed. Under the moral and political pressure of the civil rights movement, this system of second-class citizenship was officially repudiated, yet the turbulence of official integration in some cases further suppressed or destabilized the literacy assets that had developed in segregated economic and educational systems. The imbalances of this history, reaching back into the days of slavery, have never been redressed by the American body politic. We allow these imbalances to continue to organize systems of access and reward for literacy, a neglect that in fact feeds a climate for further economic and political discrimination. Although apprehended as differences in literacy rates, we really have different histories of literacy sponsorship operating in the United States—differential systems by which literacy has been subsidized, developed, and compensated.

The more that economics plays a hand in sponsoring literacy development, the more that racial discrimination in that system hurts literacy development. And in the most vicious of vicious circles, injured literacy development in turn hurts chances for economic improvement. Under practices of segregation, people of color were on the whole bypassed when subsidies started flowing in the early- and mid-twentieth century into the foundation of what would become the information economy—public and private subsidies to schools, corporations, the military, libraries, technology. As these investments helped to raise the economic value of literacy skills, further injury befell those without these skills as well as those who had the skills but could not fully cash in on their real worth. Important remedies were put in place by the major civil rights legislation of the 1960s and 1970s, uncorking the human skills and potential of African Americans and others by opening access to education and employment. However, the pace of political change around race, begrudging and backsliding, has never kept pace with economic change. Expanding civil rights and an expanding information economy have been two mighty engines going down the tracks, but they seem to be going at different speeds. Minority citizens who made later transitions into expanded schooling, intellectual labor, and political rights did not have much time to stabilize this base before the value of new opportunities was overtaken by a high-tech economy in overdrive—one that was exploiting the earlier investments in education and human capital that had gone more regularly into the white population. The economy no longer was waiting around for education to accumulate over two or three generations, as it had for typical white families in slower-moving eras of the recent past. Neither was it investing evenly in the productive potential of all citizens. Many people of color were left in cities where "work disappeared" (Wilson, 1997) and ailing tax bases meant smaller investments in human development, especially schooling. Other people of color, as in communities like mine, belong to school districts blithely organized around the interests of a white mainstream, whose children sit atop two, three, sometimes four generations of college education. As we have seen, schools (and other institutions) embed into their literacy standards and practices histories of economic transformation that not all of the students who must depend on the school have been a part of. Out of this discrepancy arise conditions of unequal access to literacy in the ostensibly democratic school. Many learners in America, some new to the society, must now achieve high standards in reading and writing without the economic and political entitlements—past and present—that are tacit to those standards. Yet still the race goes on (see Fox, 1999).

American public schools and universities have not adequately confronted the tensions inherent in the recent transformations in literacy, especially the insatiable appetite of capitalism for more, better, faster, cheaper literates. Although always accommodating to the dominant economy, schools were designed as the quintessential bearers of an earlier literacy—traditional, integrative, local, and, in some regards, democratic. Now schools strain to assimilate into their traditional practices elements of a new ideology of literacy that attacks them at their foundation. At one level, this registers as a problem of being out of date, of promulgating old ways and old reasons for reading and writing that grow further out of step with communication experiences in the surrounding society. At another level, it registers as a problem of institutional confusion and vulnerability as new demands are stacked on top of old ones and as ideologies of older literacy campaigns are appropriated by new interests. As some politicians and business leaders call for market takeover of American education, we see how, perhaps for the first time in history, the institution of the school has gotten out of step with the dominant ideology of literacy.

In closing I would like to address those readers who are committed to democracy in public education and are trying to think through this juncture in the history of literacy and schooling. By charter, democratic institutions exist to rebalance injustice—to make sure that differences in health, inheritance, origin of birth, and other inequalities do not overdetermine one's chances for liberty and quality of life. Democratic institutions serve this function by actively expanding the control that individuals have over the decisions that affect their lives and by making sure that collective resources and individual rights are equal to all members. Many forces interfere with the mission of democratic institutions, of course. In this society, government and schools too often are just another site where struggles over resources (in this case, public ones) are waged and won by those with more political and economic advantage. But as market pressures on the school intensify, it is important to remember that things are not supposed to be that way. As democratic institutions, schools are supposed to exist to offset imbalances that market philosophy helps to create—including, especially, imbalances in the worth of people's literacy. The more the school organizes literacy teaching and learning to serve the needs of the economic system, the more it betrays its democratic possibilities.

Free public education came into being because of the interdependency of an informed citizenry, a free press, and the right to vote. Citizens needed free access to information and, presumably, comparable access to the same information. This link between literacy and democracy has grown more complicated yet also more vital. As big business encouraged big government, more and more interaction was conducted through or alongside print. These developments brought new advantages to literacy skills as they enabled people with them to be more effective in systems that ran on them. In a so-called documentary society (Smith, 1974), literacy—especially of a certain sort—allowed some people to amplify their rights over the rights of others. Those who could write (or could hire writers) potentially had more ways to activate and exercise free speech. . . .

What I try to suggest here is that the new economic order presents American literacy educators with a much bigger agenda than increasing the productivity of future workers. From all angles—policy to pedagogy—literacy needs to be addressed in a civil rights context. Understanding—not just accommodating—economic and technological change is a vital responsibility of a democratic school. What is the meaning of an informed citizenry in these times? What problems are posed to First Amendment rights by inequitable access to communication technologies? How do schools validate, preserve, amplify, and equalize all routes to literacy, especially when those routes are undergoing devaluation or destruction by economic change? How might "literacy standards" be expanded to address not just individual performers but all the forces and agents that sponsor (and profit from) literacy? That is, how might we begin to talk about the responsibilities that this economy has to teachers and students instead of only the responsibility that teachers and students have to this economy?

How would the democratic mission be strengthened if students learned to read and write as forms of civil rights? My hunch is that literacy achievement would rise. Literacy's link to democracy ran as a recessive thread throughout the lives of the people I interviewed. . . . Teaching literacy in a civil rights context could bring the relevance of the school into the lives of students most often alienated from the present system—students of color, of poverty, of political asylum. Starting with the twentieth century, literacy has increasingly been captured for the cause of private wealth. It is time for the public school to reclaim in a serious way the role of literacy in strengthening democracy. Maybe the school can put to good use its slowness to change, its long memory, its entitlement to local control. As the society's major repository of the history of literacy, the school can serve to stabilize literacy learning and use its formidable resources to augment—beyond the needs of the market—the value of all the pluralistic forms of literacy that enter there.

It is easy to acknowledge the escalating standards for literacy achievement that the new economic order demands: the relatively high level of symbol skill and educational experience presumed in many of the good-paying jobs that are being created. It is harder to be mindful that the conditions giving rise to our current literacy problems also are the conditions in which these problems are experienced and the conditions in which they must be addressed. We should see not only that people must adapt to changes in expectations for literacy but also wonder how they manage it while the social systems that sustain literacy themselves undergo dramatic assault. We should not only appreciate that standards for literacy achievement keep rising but also examine what is behind that escalation: how games of economic competition—the wins, losses, and draws—destabilize the value of existing literacy skills such that "the literacy crisis" becomes chronic. We should not only appreciate the benefits of parents reading to their children but also acknowledge the complex demands on teaching and learning when knowledge, skills, and the communication systems they ride along all change even faster than children do. We should not only recognize how stigmatized groups go about accumulating literacy despite discrimination but also dedicate the resources of the democratic school more wholeheartedly to their cause. Above all, in matters of literacy, we should consider the problem not only of deficit but of surplus. This includes acknowledging the ideological congestion that hangs at the scenes of literacy learning and forms much of the mystery in learning to read and write. It also includes acknowledging how often the literacy skills that exist in American lives languish for lack of adequate sponsorship.

References

Cremin, Lawrence A. "The Cachophony of Teaching." In *Popular Education and Its Discontents.* New York: Harper & Row, 1990.

Fox, Tom. *Defending Access: A Critique of Standards in Higher Education.* Portsmouth, N.H.: Heinemann, 1999.

Gilmore, William J. *Reading Becomes a Necessity of Life: Material and Cultural Life in Rural New England* 1780–1835. Knoxville: University of Tennessee Press, 1989.

Graff, Harvey J. *The Literacy Myth: Cultural Integration and Social Structure in the Nineteenth Century.* New York: Academic Press, 1979.

Kaestle, Carl F., and others *Literacy in the United States: Readers and Reading Since 1880.* New Haven, Conn.: Yale University Press, 1991.

Martin, Henri. *The History and Power of Writing.* (L. G.Conchrane, trans.). Chicago: University of Chicago Press, 1994.

Polanyi, Karl. *The Great Transformation: The Political and Economic Origins of Our Time.* Boston: Beacon, 1944.

Smith, Dorothy. "The Social Construction of Documentary Reality." *Social Inquiry,* 1974, *44,* 313–337.

Soltow, Lee, and Stevens, Edward. *The Rise of Literacy and the Common School in the United States: A Socioeconomic Analysis to 1870.* Chicago: University of Chicago Press, 1981

Wilson, William Julius. *When Work Disappears: The World of the New Urban Poor.* New York: Vintage, 1997.

APPENDIX: INTERVIEW SCRIPT

Demographic Questions

Date of birth
Place of birth
Place of rearing
Gender/racial identity
Type of household (childhood)
Type of household (current)
Great grandparents' schooling and occupation (if known)
Grandparents' schooling and occupation (if known)
Parents'/guardians' schooling and occupation (if known)
Names and locations of all schools attended
Other training
Degrees, dates of graduation, size of graduating class
Past/present/future occupations

Source: Deborah Brandt, *Literacy in American Lives,* New York: Cambridge University Press, 2001, pp. 208–210. Reprinted with permission of Cambridge University Press.

Early Childhood Memories

Earliest memories of seeing other people writing/reading
Earliest memories of self writing/reading
Earliest memories of direct or indirect instruction
Memories of places where writing/reading occurred
Occasions associated with writing/reading
People associated with writing/reading
Organizations associated with writing/reading
Materials available for writing/reading
Ways materials entered households
Kinds of materials used
Role of technologies

Writing and Reading in School

Earliest memories of writing/reading in school
Memories of kinds of writing/reading done in school
Memories of direct instruction
Memories of self-instruction
Memories of peer instruction
Memories of evaluation
Uses of assignments/other school writing and reading
Audiences of school-based writing
Knowledge drawn on to complete assignments
Resources draw on to complete assignments
Kinds of materials available for school-based writing/teaching
Kinds of materials used
Role of technologies

Writing and Reading with Peers

Memories of sharing writing and reading
Memories of writing to/with friends

Memories of writing and reading in play
Memories of seeing friends writing and reading
Memories of reading friends' writing

Extracurricular Writing and Reading

Organizations or activities that involved writing and reading
Writing contests, pen pals, etc.

Self-Initiated Writing and Reading

Purposes for writing and reading at different stages
Genres
Audiences/uses
Teaching/learning involved

Writing on the Job

(Same questions as above)

Civic or Political Writing

Memories of initiating—written contact with government representatives, letters to editor, writing in connection with membership in civic or political organizations

Influential People

Memories of people who had a hand in one's learning to write and read

Influential Events

Significant events in the process of learning to write and read
Relative importance of writing and reading

Motivations
Consequences

Current Uses of Reading and Writing

All reading and writing done in the six months prior to the interview

Sense of Literacy Learning

Interviewee's own sense of how he or she learned to read and write
Sense of how people in general learn to read and write

QUESTIONS FOR REFLECTION

1. Using the interview script as a guide (see Appendix), write your own literacy autobiography. How did you learn how to write? How did you learn how to read? How did a competition among the sponsors of your literacy affect your experience?
2. Interview someone who is at least ten years older or ten years younger than you. What do you notice about how their literacy learning experience compares to yours? What might account for the similarities or differences?
3. What does Brandt mean by "accumulating literacy"? How might "accumulating literacy" estrange teachers and students? How might it connect them?
4. How do literacy resources circulate in the school where you work? Who has access to what?
5. In his interview with Brandt, David Karem quotes from the conclusion of *Literacy in American Lives:* "As democratic institutions, schools are supposed to exist to offset imbalances that market philosophy helps to create, including especially imbalances in the worth of people's literacy. The more that the school organizes literacy teaching and learning to serve the

needs of the economic system, the more it betrays its democratic possibilities. The more that private interests take over the education and development of our young citizens, the less of a democracy we have." What is your view of this assertion and why?

6. What might literacy in American lives look like at the end of the twenty-first century? What practices or values are likely to endure? Which might not?

INDEX

This page represents a continuation of the copyright page.

THE AUTHOR

Deborah Brandt is a professor of English at the University of Wisconsin–Madison, where she teaches undergraduate writing and graduate courses in literacy and contemporary writing theory. Her research focuses on the changing conditions for literacy learning in late-twentieth-century and early-twenty-first-century American society. She is the author of two previous books: *Literacy as Involvement: The Acts of Writers, Readers, and Texts,* which won the 1993 David H. Russell Award for Distinguished Research from the National Council of Teachers of English; and *Literacy in American Lives,* which, in addition to winning the 2003 Grawemeyer Award, also won the 2002 Mina P. Shaughnessy Award from the Modern Language Association and the 2003 Outstanding Book Award from the Conference on College Composition and Communication.

TITLES IN THE JOSSEY-BASS
OUTSTANDING IDEAS IN EDUCATION SERIES

What I Learned in School
Reflections on Race, Child Development, and School Reform

By James P. Comer

What I Learned in School highlights, in a single source, the major contributions of world-renowned scholar Dr. James P. Comer, whose visionary work has dramatically shaped the fields of school reform, child development, psychology, and race.

This collection is beautifully arranged and includes an introduction and engaging updates from the author that paint a remarkable picture of what we've all learned so far, and what we all must learn going forward. The excerpts span Dr. Comer's career—from his best-selling book *Maggie's American Dream* to the influential *Leave No Child Behind*.

JAMES P. COMER, MD, MPH is the Maurice Falk Professor of Child Psychiatry at the Yale University School of Medicine's Child Study Center. The author of numerous books, including *Leave No Child Behind*, he is perhaps best known for founding the Comer School Development Program. In 2007, he received the Grawemeyer Award in education.

ISBN: 978-0-470-40771-4 • Hardcover